ISBN 978-1-330-94557-5
PIBN 10124771

1 MONTH OF
FREE
READING

at

www.ForgottenBooks.com

By purchasing this book you are eligible for one month membership to ForgottenBooks.com, giving you unlimited access to our entire collection of over 700,000 titles via our web site and mobile apps.

To claim your free month visit:

www.forgottenbooks.com/free124771

English
Français
Deutsche
Italiano
Español
Português

www.forgottenbooks.com

Mythology Photography **Fiction**
Fishing Christianity **Art** Cooking
Essays Buddhism Freemasonry
Medicine **Biology** Music **Ancient
Egypt** Evolution Carpentry Physics
Dance Geology **Mathematics** Fitness
Shakespeare **Folklore** Yoga Marketing
Confidence Immortality Biographies
Poetry **Psychology** Witchcraft
Electronics Chemistry History **Law**
Accounting **Philosophy** Anthropology
Alchemy Drama Quantum Mechanics
Atheism Sexual Health **Ancient History**
Entrepreneurship Languages Sport
Paleontology Needlework Islam
Metaphysics Investment Archaeology
Parenting Statistics Criminology
Motivational

STUDIES IN DREAMS

BY

MARY ARNOLD-FORSTER

(MRS. H. O. ARNOLD-FORSTER)

WITH A FOREWORD BY

MORTON PRINCE, M.D., LL.D.

Author of "The Nature of Mind and Human Automatism,
"The Unconscious," "The Dissociation of a
Personality," etc.

New York

THE MACMILLAN COMPANY

1921

0 4 2 0 9

TO
KA

FOREWORD

I have been asked by the dreamer of these dreams to add a foreword of my own. I do not know that I can add anything that will contribute to their interest, whether in the way of discussion, criticism, or interpretation. The author of the book modestly makes no claim to be a scientific explorer but only to be a recorder of her own dream experiences, who has been impelled "to stray a little beyond the province" assigned and "to attempt some partial explanation of the riddles that are met with." But the reader, I am sure, will find that she has scarcely done herself justice in this diffident attitude, for the accurate recording of observations accurately made is the basis of science and requires the development and possession of no common talent. Such observations are of much more scientific value than a number of inadequate theories—inadequate because based upon only a selected or limited group of facts. Moreover, these pages are rich in sound comments and discussions of the recorded phenomena, which are suggestive of new problems and points of view, and the author offers us particularly a well-considered new theory of the mechanism of dreams. A considerable number of the observations recorded must be regarded as additions to our knowledge and as new data for an adequate interpretation of the mechanism of dreams. Besides the recording of her own experiences, Mrs. Arnold-Forster sets before herself as her main task that of finding out "by experiment and careful observation all that we can learn about the working of the various mental faculties in the dream state"—reason, memory, will, imagination. As the parts played by these mental processes obviously bear upon the various theories which have been proposed for the explanation of dreams, the results of the author's study of her own dreams must be regarded as an original contribution to the subject. The interesting theory which she proposes (Chapter IX) is one that deserves careful consideration. The unprejudiced reader who has not already accepted one of the current theories of dreams will be attracted by the diffidence and freedom from dogmatism of the author, and will study these pages with greater open-mindedness from knowing that she is thoroughly versed in the mass of literature on dreams which has accumulated in recent years, and has tested the theories in the light of her own observations. Mrs. Arnold-Forster, therefore, is no amateur. I venture to think, however, that most professional psychologists will not share the "respect and natural awe" which, with charming modesty, she avows for the "vast library of books" in which are embodied the results of the so-called scientific investigations which have been stimulated by the present-day medical interest in dreams. More likely they look upon such "scientific'' results as—pipe dreams or cigarette dreams.

The quality of the interest of the reader in this book will undoubtedly be largely determined by his previous attitude of mind towards dreams and their interpretation. If he has a closed mind, has already committed himself towards some theory of dream mechanism—and I fear many students of present-day psychology already have—if he thinks he already knows it all, his interest may be hypercritically modified by the limitation of the task which the author has set before herself. I am not sure that this contribution has not gained by this limitation. We have theories in plenty of the mechanisms by which dreams are excited and worked out by some or other part of the mind, but none is wholly satisfactory, none, at least, is universally applicable to all dreams. We have physiological theories and psychological theories: we have theories making use of unconscious processes and conscious processes, of symbolisms, and double-faced Janus-like processes—an underlying latent and a manifest conscious process: and we have theories of naughty and disguised wishes, and a watchful prude of a censor that spoils all the fun of dreaming and lets us fulfil our concealed wishes only on condition we don't know: we have what we want, and therefore can't consciously enjoy forbidden fruit even in dreams: and we have theories of haphazard and ''trial and error'' processes, and many more. But all are theories, and nothing is proven fact. Some, nevertheless, work out very well with certain dreams, and then, when we try to apply them to other dreams, they won't work. No universally applicable theory has yet been invented. I do not know why any one theory of dream mechanism should be true for all dreams· as well hold that the mechanism of all conscious thought is the same; that, for instance, because some of our problems are solved subconsciously, all are; that, because some of our antipathies, some likes and dislikes, some fears and some kinds of behaviour are determined by hidden subconscious motives, all are; or, conversely, that because many or most problems are solved consciously, all are; or that, because many motives stand out blatantly in the broad daylight of consciousness, none are hidden in the subconscious; or that, because most behaviour is determined by conscious intent or feeling, all is; or, again, because some actions are instinctive and determined by inherited mechanisms, that all behaviour is determined by such performed instincts; and, conversely, that, because most behaviour is due to acquired dispositions, all is due to such mechanisms; and so on.

The fact is, Mrs. Arnold-Forster hits the nail on the head when she says "there are dreams and dreams, and we must get rid of the assumption that they all resemble each other" This assumption is a very common one: in particular it is often assumed that a dream implies incongruity, or incoherence, or the grotesque, or logical anarchy. Dreams, as the author stresses, may not only exhibit orderly imagination, and reasoning, and memory, and other quali-

ties of the mind, but this imagination, reasoning and
memory may be highly constructive, ingeniously inventive, and produce imaginings or romances comparable in structure and sequence of ideas to stories
of fiction or real life evolved by the same waking
mind. This seems to be particularly the case with
the dreams of the author, who therefore delights in
her dream life and finds an enchanting recreation
therein after the cares of the day, as the lover of
novels, who reads into the wee hours of the night,
finds refreshment from the strain of the day's work.
Mr. Greenwood (quoted by Mrs. Arnold-Forster)
finds his dreams of the same high imaginative order
and takes the same enjoyment in the dreaming of
them: and so have many others.

What is still needed, as the author has pointed out,
is systematic and accurate recording of their dreams
by many persons, and the correlation of the phenomena with identical phenomena occurring in certain other states of the waking mental life. If this
were done, we should be surprised to find what a
great variety of forms and structure dreams have,
how greatly they differ in type, and in the mental
processes involved. We thus should have the material from which we could safely construct theories
of mechanisms that would satisfy the different types.
After the collection of this varied material, we could
then begin, with greater safety, to analyse and interpret. In some we should find symbolism, in
others none; in some repressed wishes, in others
unrepressed wishes, or fears, doubts, and scruples;

in some sex urgings, in others the urgings of one
or more of the other various innate instincts which
are the prime movers of human behaviour; in some
the solution of problems which have baffled our
waking consciousness, in others the mere illogical
fantasies of a weak, dissociated extract of our mental selves; in some the reproduction of memories,
and living over again in realistic form previous
actual experiences, in others imaginary episodes or
apparent super-knowledge constructed out of previous information; in some incongruous, grotesque
phantasmagoria in cinema-like scenes, in others romances or well-constructed fantasies requiring for
their invention a large system of thought and an intelligence and imagination comparable to the waking
self-consciousness. And in some we should find that
the dream, as in waking life, is only the manifested
expression of deeper-lying subconscious processes;
and in some, probably in most, that it is just what
it appears to be—nothing more.

⌐ The drawback to such collections, apart from the
rareness of the capacity to remember and record
accurately, would be, I fear, the dullness of reading
them. The emotional tones which give the pleasure
or induce the anguish of the dream in the dreamer
cannot be reproduced in a verbal record; nor do they
always correspond to the dream action or images,
and hence no description can reproduce them. They
are integral elements of the personal self which con-
tributes them. The study of dream collections
would appeal only to the psychologist, and then only

to one specially interested in such mental phenomena. Every one, we can safely say, is not endowed with the gift of imagination to dream such delightful romances, tales of adventure, and fantasies in general as the gifted dreamer of these dreams, who finds in her nightly pilgrimages "into the enchanted country that lies beyond" a release from the toil of the day and compensation for "the sad and anxious waking hours" that "life brings to all of us." Undoubtedly, as the author tells us, this dream imagination has been cultivated, and can be cultivated and directed, to a certain extent, by any one who has the persistence and desire. But a natively endowed and cultured imagination is probably essential as a prerequisite for romance of a high order, as it is for analogous feats by the waking self. We see what is practically the same phenomenon manifested in waking life, not by that system of thought called the "self" or self-consciousness, but by a shunted-off, dissociated system which has gained its liberty and acquired independent activity.

Such a system is commonly called subconscious, but it is subconscious only because the "self" is still awake. Let the "self" go to sleep, or be put to sleep by some hypnotic or other device, and the shunted-off system, escaping from its subterranean prison, is now dominant, is indeed a self, free to romance as it pleases. But before, while still shut-up, or perhaps it were better expressed shut-out, of the awareness of the self-consciousness, it was free to indulge in imaginings without much restraint, much as the prisoners confined and forgotten in the French Bastille were free to indulge their imagination in romances though other liberty was denied them. I have quite a collection of written romances, written by a subconscious self while within its own Bastille, and songs and music and the invention of a strange new logistic language have not failed to find a mode of expression. True subconscious dreams they are, fabricated by a newly constellated mental system that was reconstructed out of the self-conscious or personal system—out of the jetsam and flotsam of conscious experiences; the discarded, or forgotten, or repressed memories, wishes, ideas, and imaginings.

I am unable to see that such a system and its fabrications differ in principle from the "Dream Mind," as Mrs. Arnold-Forster aptly calls it, and its fabrications. Both may, and at times do, have their own respective subconscious processes butting in, modifying or determining their dreams.

Furthermore, both kinds of dreams can be cultivated, directed, and to a large extent controlled. (Mrs. Arnold-Forster has shown how she has learned to "control" her own dreams, and I may add to hers the testimony of experimentally controlled dreams in one of my subjects by suggestion even to the extent of directing the theme of the dream.)[1] Simple commonplace subconscious writings, the vaporings of the ouija board, the so-called trance state and the fabrications of spiritualistic "mediums" may be,

[1] "The Unconscious," The Macmillan Co., p. 197.

and generally are, nothing more than ''subconscious'' day-dreams, manifestations of subconscious memories identical in principle with normal nocturnal dreams. These subconscious dreams, it is well known, can be cultivated; which means that out of almost any material of the mind—memories, emotional impulses and instincts, acquired dispositions, etc.—a self-functioning system can be constellated and educated into a subconscious system manifesting itself in day-dreams. It is common experience that the more such manifestations are practised and encouraged to become a habit, the more readily they occur and the more highly developed becomes the intelligence of the system.

I mention this as only one illustration of the data which can be obtained from abnormal and experimental psychology, for the understanding of dream processes. I doubt if there is a single phenomenon observed in dreams, or peculiarity of the work of the dream mind, that is not also to be found in other conditions than sleep. I mean conditions, whether artificially produced or the abnormal resultant of intrinsic psychological processes, where the mind is dissociated as it is in sleep. By correlating dream phenomena with analogous phenomena found in these other conditions and studying the mechanisms and essential characteristics of the abnormal and artificial groups, particularly by the experimental method, we can obtain an insight into and understanding of the normal dream mind. The study of abnormal psychology—including its variant pro-

duced by artifice—has thrown more light on the
workings of the normal mind than all the centuries
of academic studies of the latter.

Mrs. Arnold-Forster directs attention to certain
characteristics of memory and imagination in
dreams (Chapter V). The former is remarkable
for the wealth and distinctness of detail with which
former scenes and experiences are reproduced; indeed, it may be, visualised with a vividness equal to
reality. Even momentary experiences which originally were merely fugitive impressions, casually
attended to, may reappear in wonderful detail and
distinctness as the material of dreams.

This feat of memory is not peculiar to dreams,
but may be correlated with the same phenomenon
manifested by the trance mind and other dissociated
states of consciousness.[1] In "crystal visions" we
have it in a more or less isolated form. Likewise
the heightening of the imagination and its freedom
from the restrictions of time and space, which Mrs.
Arnold-Forster interestingly dwells upon, find their
analogues in dissociated states of mind other than
sleep. It would be easy to cite examples of the day-
dreamer or trance-dreamer in whose fantasies "distance is annihilated" and centuries passed over in
the twinkling of an eye. As in normal dreams, the
soul may seem to leave the body and hover in space
or be transported to another sphere—celestial or
cosmic.

In similar fashion I might point out that in such

[1] "The Unconscious," Section II.

states are found the analogues of other dream phenomena, such as symbolisms, the solution of problems—mathematical and personal—literary manifestations of creative imagination, ascribed by Robert Louis Stevenson to his "Brownies" somewhere
beneath or outside the dream mind, the doubling of
the conscious self (manifested by the activity of a
second consciousness, or the "Guide" in the author's
dreams—Chapter XIII), defence reactions, visions,
and other hallucinations.

So, though normal dreams are of value for the
light they throw on the phenomena of abnormal
psychology, still more the manifold and varied data
of the latter, the larger field and subject to experi-
mentation, give an understanding of the former.
This is the reverse of the point of view of the
Freudian psychology. The latter subjects itself to
the errors and fallacies necessarily arising from the
acceptation of, and dogmatic adherence to, a theory
which is true of only particular types of dreams, and
therefore limited in its applications.

Not the least interesting as well as novel of the
dream phenomena recorded by the author are those
of "dream control" and flying dreams. The fact
that Mrs. Arnold-Forster has succeeded in controlling her dreams, at least to the extent of pro-
hibiting unpleasant dreams, and teaching herself to
fly, will be a novel contribution to most students.
Both phenomena have interesting corollaries: the
former involves the implication of the principles of
doubling of consciousness and the "censor," and the

latter of dissociation of all sensory impressions including what is known as cœnesthesia, or the organic sensations streaming from the viscera and other parts of the body. At least so flying dreams can be explained. If we assume that all such sensations are completely dissociated from the dream mind, so that the latter become pure thought and images (for there is evidence that during ordinary sleep such impressions are still received), we have a mental condition suitable for the creative imagination to fabricate the illusion of flying, untrammelled by any conflict with sensory impressions of reality. Mrs. Arnold-Forster, herself, has apparently experienced such a dream without the flying illusion, judging from her description (p. 151). Such complete dissociation of all consciousness of the body finds its analogue, as I have observed, in a waking dissociated state, in which the subject describes herself as just "thought in space" without a body.

Given such a dissociation, it would theoretically only require a creative imagination with vivid imagery to fabricate the illusions or hallucinations of objective flying. The mind is capable of creating almost any kind of hallucination even to the extent of shaking hands with an imaginary "spirit," provided it is not contradicted by the conflicting awareness of reality.

It is insisted by those who hold certain theories regarding the mechanism of dreams, particularly by the school of psycho-analysts, that their theories are "purely inductive, being built up" (as a brilliant expounder writes) "step by step on the basis of actual experiences without the introduction of any *a priori* speculative hypotheses " Conceding this, and disregarding the fact that many of the alleged facts of experience are actually not facts but interpretations of facts, it still remains true that the same can be said for contending theories. Each is an inductively reached conclusion. The explanation of such differing theories is that each is based on different facts of experience. All theories as well as hypotheses of science hold good only until newly discovered facts require reconsideration and new explanations. Thus the older theories of atoms and the ultimate nature of matter held good until the discovery of new facts required a re-examination of the theories and a new formulation of conceptions in terms of electrons and electricity. And so with the biological theories which in consequence of the discoveries of Darwin and Mendel had to be chucked overboard or recast.

The claim for any theory of dreams based on its having been preached inductively cannot be very impressive. Mrs. Arnold-Forster brings to our attention types of dreams which she finds herself unable to fit in with present-day fashionable theories. It is interesting to note that after subjecting her dreams to self psycho-analysis she fails to find that they substantiate the Freudian theory that all dreams are symbolic, and still more "that they are all symbols of repressed desire"—and particularly sex wishes. Without denying the occurrence of symbolism, according to her interpretation this symbolism is for the most part "of a simple and direct nature relating the dream to some mood that I have experienced, or some problem that I have met with, and it is often fairly easy to trace this idea which the dream represents in an allegorical form. In this modified sense it seems evident that many dreams are symbolical."

Mrs. Arnold-Forster, as a student of Freud and his followers and thoroughly grounded in the Freudian literature, recognises that the true psycho-analyst would not be content with such an interpretation; and that, according to the Freudian theory, it is impossible to be one's own psycho-analyst because of the self-censorship exerted by the mind against such revelations—shall we say against facing oneself and the hidden truths of self. For my part I am much more impressed by Mrs. Arnold-Forster's simple interpretations of her dreams (of which she gives illustrations), perhaps because they fit in with my own studies, than I am with those interpretations to which they are exposed by the Freudian theory (as the author of these dreams fully realises). Surely the wider and more intensive our experience the more must we sympathise with the plea expressed in these pages "for the exercise of sober judgment and common sense in our study of this subject and the conclusions we form."

To those engaged in the study of the purely psychological problems involved in dreams, the author's conception of the mental mechanisms by which

dreams are constructed will be of interest (Chapter
IX). Mrs. Arnold-Forster proposes an explanation
of dream construction which is as ingenious as it
is simple. The mechanism is that of association of
ideas with the co-operation of the imagination.
Illustrations of how this mechanism works are given
in two specific dreams recorded.· The apparent
incoherence and inconsecutiveness of many dreams
is attributed to the failure of memory after waking
to recall the connecting links necessary to make the
dream coherent. In dream building, if I understand
the theory correctly, one idea calls up another by
successive association—free association, unham-
pered by critical and discriminating judgment, which
in the normal process of thinking rejects those associated ideas which are not acceptable or germane
to the subject in hand. The dream imagination
then seizes upon certain elements in the associated
idea, intensifies and objectifies them in imagery by
which, for instance, objects are vividly visualised.
Thus, in one dream, a winding path in a landscape
suggests by association a railroad, which is at once
visualised also in the landscape. The two crossing
each other suggests a railroad crossing, which is in
turn visualised; then follows the idea of danger from
a possible approaching train, and, presto! the sound
of such an onrushing train is heard; and so on, one
association calling up another to be vividly represented in images and worked by imagination into a
connected story, the images suggesting thoughts and
vice versa. The whole is very much like the process

of certain types of thinking carried on when awake by day, "only at night the imagination is not fettered by the discipline which restrains our wandering thoughts from following too eagerly in the random track of every chance thought or suggestion. The imagination in sleep, unchecked in this way, can devote itself to perfecting each successive image that arises, giving life and reality to each in turn, metamorphosing them often, and constantly adding new facts and fresh touches to the pictures which are its creation."

It is curious and may be interesting to note that Mrs. Arnold-Forster's theory is supported by the testimony of a co-conscious personality which I had occasion to study. It is well known that a number of cases, in which a secondary co-conscious personality claimed to be awake while the principal personality was dreaming, have been observed. In the Beauchamp case the co-conscious personality, observing the dreams as they occurred, testified that during sleep sensory stimuli (sounds, the touch of the bed-clothes, etc.) are received and " 'make sensory images or impressions in the same way as in the daytime.' These weave themselves into dreams, but they also recall memories of what she has seen and heard and read, in fact everything that she has ever been conscious of, so that in this way they arouse connected dreams." [1]

This theory of the dream mechanism which Mrs. Arnold-Forster proposes will probably be regarded

[1] "The Dissociation of a Personality," p. 329.

by psychologists as one of the most important of
the contributions contained in her book. It is, as
she points out, in entire opposition to the Freudian
conception, leaving "entirely out of account the sort
of hidden meaning that the psycho-analyst finds in
dreams," as well as the symbolism and unconscious
sex wishes. In other passages, however, the author
fully recognises that there may be dreams, especially
those of morbid persons, to which the Freudian
theory applies. She has only to do with her own
experiences. I, for one, am strongly inclined to believe that her theory is a sound interpretation at
least of a certain type of dream, and may, perhaps,
govern the majority of dreams. Probably Mrs.
Arnold-Forster will agree that in other types less
emphasis should be placed on the associative process
and more on the *creative* imagination as contrasted
with what, perhaps, I may call the *passive* imagination, the slave of associated ideas: the creative
imagination thinks out, reasons, foresees, arranges
and composes according to a conceived plan, and is
not the slave of associated ideas.

In some of the dreams recorded by the author,
flying dreams for instance, it seems to me that the
creative imagination is conspicuous and dominates
the associative process. Certainly there are dreams,
as might be illustrated from my own collection (not
personal experiences), in which there is an argument, the end is foreseen and the whole is a well-
worked-out story or allegory. No associative process alone could have produced such logical coherence.

In such dreams the motivating dispositions which have determined the theme and inspired the creative imagination are another matter and are to be searched for in the antecedent conscious life of the individual.

I am influenced in this notion by what I conceive to be the analogues of night-dreams, namely, the fantasies of other dissociated states—day-dreaming and subconscious dreaming. In these two conditions I have observed dreams substantially indentical with those occurring during sleep, but although associated ideas may have suggested the motives inspiring the theme and otherwise been factors, the creative imagination has worked as it does in the composition of romance. I have already referred to this phenomenon. The fact is that all depends upon that organisation of the dissociated mental systems which is called by Mrs. Arnold-Forster the dream mind, whether functioning when asleep, when awake, or when subconscious. When these systems are so highly organised as to be capable of reason, imagination and will, and when they include the so-called instincts—when, in other words, they constitute an "Intelligence"—they are capable of working in a way comparable to that of the waking intelligence. But when the senses are eliminated, and when therefore cognition of reality is also eliminated —as in sleep—there is necessarily a corresponding limitation of that adjustment and correlation of thought to reality which is one of the essential qualities of dreams. Undoubtedly the dream mind, like

all dissociated systems, can be educated into a highly
organised intelligence. This seems to have been
the case, I venture to think, with the dream mind of
the author as well as with that of some of the recorders of dreams cited in this book.

From this point of view there must be as many
different types of dreams as there are types of organised mental systems: even the Freudian mechanisms, of which I believe I have seen examples,[1]
should occur.

As Mrs. Arnold-Forster says, "dreams are not
all alike, but are as manifold in their nature as are
the thoughts and imaginations of men"; and, I may
add, dreams vary not only in their nature but also
in their mechanisms, just as do the mental systems
of human personality, whether they be mutilated and
dissociated or unmutilated and complete.

MORTON PRINCE.

Boston, U. S. A.

---

[1] "The Mechanism and Interpretation of Dreams," Journal of Abnormal Psychology, vol. v. No. 6 (1911).

PREFACE

We are somewhat more than ourselves in our sleeps, and the slumber of the body seems to be but the waking of the soul. It is the litigation of sense, but the liberty of reason; and our waking conceptions do not match the fancies of our sleeps.—Sir Thomas Browne, *Religio Medici,* xi.

The following slight studies dealing with certain dream problems have been written from a series of notes, in which dreams and certain experiments in dreaming have been more or less regularly recorded during a long period of years. If it is asked what they have to offer that is new on a subject on which so much has been already written, the answer must be that we are even now only at the beginning of this study, that many problems concerning dreams and concerning the border state that lies between sleeping and waking are still to be solved, and that some of these have as yet hardly been touched on at all in the literature of dreams. There are many aspects of these questions which can only be very imperfectly dealt with by an unscientific observer whose want of technical knowledge is a grave disadvantage in writing on a subject to which so much learning has been devoted, yet I believe that there is room in this fascinating study not only for the philosopher and the psychologist, but also for the unlearned but faithful recorder of personal experience. Our dreams are the most individual of all our experiences, and we each approach them from a separate standpoint of our own. Psychology is the science of individual experience, and the facts that are eventually sifted and weighed in its laboratories must first be gathered by humble gleaners in many widely scattered fields.

The plea made in this book that more of us should learn to watch and record accurately the facts of our own dream experience is made, not only because of the constantly increasing value to science of a fuller knowledge of the working of the dream mind, but also because I am sure that those who follow this study and learn to remember more of their own dream life, will find themselves amply rewarded. Life brings to all of us sad and anxious waking hours, and to most men it brings days of monotonous labour; but to every one, whatever the sorrow or the toil of the day may be, night should bring release. When we enter the country of dreams we are not only liberated from the bondage of labour, but shackles are loosed which by day keep the imagination tied to earth. Only in sleep the imagination is set at liberty and is free to exercise its fullest powers. Sleep which brings us our dreams fulfils the eternal need within us, the need of romance, the need of adventure; for sleep is the gate which lets us slip through into the enchanted country that lies beyond. We give too little heed to the nightly miracle of our dreams. Long hours are spent by us in dreaming sleep, during which we are absorbed in a life which is for the most part forgotten or ignored by our waking consciousness. We speak of it so rarely to each other that we know hardly anything about each other's dream life, and many things combine to make us curiously ignorant and forgetful even of our own. For want of interest in dreams, or merely because we have never learned how to retain these fugitive impressions, they vanish when we wake as mist vanishes in sunlight. Nothing fades more quickly than these memories, and unless some method is acquired by which we can hold them fast they are lost; but if a more alert interest were once aroused this need not happen, and we need not so often lose the recollection of all that has filled the sleeping hours. As we learn to use more intelligently the instruments of mind and body that are ours, our interest is quickened in the processes of dreaming, and in the working of the mind in sleep. Such quickened observation means for us the heightening of consciousness, the becoming aware of new experience—and "to become aware of new experience is one of the thrills life gives us." [1] A twofold pleasure then becomes ours: the interest that the study of dreams gives us and the delight of dream adventures, a delight that I have discovered, can be greatly extended and perfected by learning how to dream well. Amongst the records of dreams that have made the foundation of this book, a considerable number are notes of experiments which were

[1] Stephen Graham, "A Tramp's Sketches."

made to find out to what extent the control of our dreams lies within our power; how, for instance, dreams of distress can be checked or banished, and how far the art of happy dreaming can be cultivated. This question of dream control does not, as far as I know, come within the scope of other books. I have found it a fascinating path of enquiry, and perhaps other lovers of dreaming may be willing to find out a way along similar hitherto unmapped roads. In this company of dream lovers and dream students there are very likely explorers who have already travelled much further than I have done, whose investigations have been more thorough, and who might, if there were a clearing house of dream knowledge, bring it their stores of valuable experience.

By rights, perhaps, the task of an unscientific recorder of dreams should be simply to explore—to record his experiences in the dream state; leaving it to science to explain the whys and wherefores of what has been observed. But it is very difficult for one who has dreamed much, and thought much, and read much, about dreaming not to stray a little beyond the proper province of the recorder, and not to attempt some partial explanation of some of the riddles that are met with. Part, at least, of the extensive literature of psychology must be studied before we can attempt to formulate any answers to these questions, and as our reading extends the complexity of the problems before us deepens.

Personal experience seems often to contradict

widely accepted theories of dream construction and origin; the truth being that dreams are of such infinite variety that no theory of their mechanism, even when formulated by the greatest of teachers, will adequately account for the whole of this wide field of human experience.

In order to use the language of science correctly, the training of science is needed, and many pitfalls lie in the way of the student. One such pitfall is met with at the very outset. Scientific critics have come to no agreement as to the term that shall be used to express the "mind" or "self" which appears to operate in dreams. The existence of such a "self" or "mind" as distinct from the normal mind is indeed a matter of dispute and is accepted only as a possible working hypothesis for the purposes of enquiry. The expression "unconscious mind" is objected to as being a contradiction in terms; and the writer who, avoiding it, reverts to the word "subconscious," finds that this gives even less satisfaction. An apology must therefore be made at once for the use throughout these pages of the expression "dream mind," an expression which is no less "woolly," no less unsatisfactory than the others, and which equally evades grave fundamental difficulties, its only merit being that, as it makes no pretensions to belong to the vocabulary of science, it does not suggest the possession of scientific knowledge to which I can lay no claim.

This little book, which is too slight to take a place amongst the more learned books about dreams, will

fulfil the object with which it was written if it suc-
ceeds in showing something of the attractiveness of
this study, and if it reminds us of the measure, too
often overlooked, that is added by our dreams to the
sum of life's happiness.

CONTENTS

CHAPTER   PAGE

FOREWORD BY DR. MORTON PRINCE   vii

PREFACE   xxvii

Room in this study for lay observers and recorders as
well as for scientific investigators. Charm of dreams
and of their study. Psychology the science of individual experience. Need of a clearing house of dreams.
Question of dream-control apparently outside the scope
of other books. Difficulty for lay observers in use of
scientific terms.

I INTRODUCTORY   1

Growth of interest in this study. Scientific attitude
in the nineteenth century. Difference of present attitude. Teaching of Freud and his followers. Bergson,
F. Greenwood. Methods of the dream mind. What
faculties are active in dreams? Do any of these faculties change their character in the dream state? Does
our control over our thoughts wholly cease?

II DREAM CONTROL   22

Desirability of some form of dream control. Bad
dreams of many kinds. Dream control established by
means of a formula. Charles Lamb and dreams of
fear. Children's bad dreams. Richard Rolle the Hermit. Amulets and charms. Dream control considered
from the point of view of psycho-analysts.

III FLYING DREAMS   37

Further control of dreams. Voluntary dreaming. Ex-
tension of powers of voluntary dreaming by means of
a second formula. Experiments. Flying dreams in
war-time.

IV DREAM RECORDING   52

Memory as a dream recorder. Methods of remembering and recording dreams. Difficulty in case of dreams
of changing identity. Early morning dreams. Epictetus's warning to dreamers. An apology.

CHAPTER   PAGE

V DREAM MEMORY, DREAM IMAGINATION AND DREAM
   REASON 67

   Memory as dream builder. Imagination as dream architect. World of dreams still the familiar world
   known to us—but laws of time and space annihilated.
   Examples. Operation of reason in dreams. Good reasoning producing unsatisfactory results because dream
   reason is imperfectly supplied with necessary facts.
   Arguments in dreams.

VI THE "SUPER-DREAM" 83

   Nature of the "super-dream." Imagination undergoes
   a dream change. All faculties working at their highest capacity. Condorcet. Nevil Story-Maskelyne and
   others. H. Fabre. R. L. Stevenson. A novelist of to-
   day.

VII SYMBOLISM IN DREAMS, AND THE SIGNIFICANCE OF
    DREAMS IN TRADITION 93

   Theory of symbolic nature of dreams in modern psychology. Morton Prince's definition of dreams as "the
   symbolical expression of almost any thought." Censor
   theory. Psycho-analysis. Examples of allegorical
   dreams symbolising thoughts or moods which had occupied the mind by day. Ancient belief in the symbolic and prophetic character of dreams, and in dreams
   as channels of Divine communications with men.
   Some ancient and modern superstitions.

VIII DREAM PLACES 102

   Dream countries—Mr. E. M. Martin. Dream houses.
   Faithfulness of dream memory. De Quincey's Easter
   dream. Elia—Recurrent place dreams. Rudyard Kipling. My friend's story.

IX DREAM CONSTRUCTION 113

   Comparison between dreams and wandering day
   thoughts. Construction of dream story. In dreams
   the thing thought of visualised—made objective. Consecutiveness—reasonableness of dream story depends
   on connecting links which are easily forgotten. Examples of dream construction.

X SENSE IMPRESSIONS IN DREAMS 122

   "Sensorial" and "psychic" dreams. Part played by

CHAPTER PAGE

sensations in dreams. Havelock Ellis quoted. Flying dreams not affected by bodily position. Dreams affected by temperature of the body. Colour sense in dreams. Senses of smell and taste.

XI BORDERLAND STATE 134

Transition state between waking and sleeping described. Two stages:
(a) Earlier stage furthest removed from sleep.
(b) Later stage nearest to border-line of sleep.
Earlier stage—State of quiet. Curious experiences in this state. Possibility of telepathic communication by channels other than those of the senses. Belief that such communications may take place between the living and the dead. Sir O. Lodge. S.P.R. investigations. Distinction between experiences in dream state and in borderland state. State of quiet. Analogy with hypnotic state suggested. Also analogy with condition necessary to artist's creative work.

XII BORDERLAND STATE 150

Later stage of transition state—nearest to sleep. Visions seen in this state of the same material as our dreams. Approaching and crossing the border-line of sleep. Simultaneous working of normal and dream mind perceived. Intercepted messages. Crossing strands of thought. Heightened sensitiveness to sense impressions.

XIII THE ACTORS IN DREAMS—"THE DREAM GUIDE" . . 160

Nature of the personages who play their parts in our dreams. How do they sustain their rôles in dramatic dreams and dreams of argument? The "Guide" in my dreams. Belief that these actors are the creation of the dream mind. Consciousness of dual personality. Dreams of the dead . . . a different order of experience from experience in borderland state.

XIV MORAL SENSE IN DREAMS 173

Differences between moral sense in dreams and in normal life. Absence of sense of responsibility. Other differences. Dreams of anger, an experiment in dream control. Teaching of the Freudian school of psychoanalysts. Dream control an answer to the theory that the province of·dreams lies wholly outside our control.

STUDIES IN DREAMS

CHAPTER I

INTRODUCTORY

No process or transaction of the mind has engaged so much attention for so many centuries as our dreaming when we sleep. Long before there was any thinking about thought, there was thinking about dreams.—F. Greenwood.

From the earliest dawn of history and legend we know that men have dreamed and have told their dreams. From as remote a past interpreters were found ready to explain the significance of dreams; but it is only within the last quarter of a century that the light of modern research has been turned fully on to their study, and that, in place of the soothsayers of old, men of science of all nations have begun to analyse the frail stuff of which our dreams are made.

During the lifetime of a generation the way in which the subject is regarded has totally changed. To have ventured fifty years ago to write a book about dreams would have required moral courage, for the subject was looked upon as unworthy the consideration of serious people. To write on it to-day also requires courage, but of a wholly different kind. It is formidable now only because of the number and the learning of the books that are already written about it. This change of attitude is very noticeable if the literature of dreams in the nineteenth century is considered. Scientific men were still absorbed in the triumphs of that wonderful age of discovery in the physical world, and had hardly begun to find out how great was the work awaiting science in the field of psychology. Many of them still regarded psychology with a certain suspicion, and had not recognised that any purpose useful to science could be served by the study of the unconscious or semiconscious mind. In every generation the fields of knowledge have had to be widened and extended so as to cover new investigations, and only too often the mandarins of science have tried to bar the way of the explorer, and have condemned the impulse to push out into new regions of thought. It was not until recent years that investigation of certain secrets of man's personality, by means of the revelation of the mind in sleep, began to attract the attention of men of science, and that this new study began to throw light upon some of the difficult problems that confront the physician in dealing with the human nerves and brain.

It is no longer true, as it was when people began to study and to write about dreams in the last century, that the science of medicine approaches such an enquiry as this in a spirit of simple materialism. The interest of medical science is no longer "narrowed down into a predetermination to believe in the dissecting knife, the microscope, and the galvanic

battery, as the only interpreters of man to himself.''
No one would rest content to-day with the explanation given by Dr. Benjamin Richardson in a course
of health lectures delivered in the ''eighties,'' when
he told his hearers to banish from their minds the
idea that there was anything in dreams that was not
to be explained by purely physical causes. He
showed how dreams arose from disturbances communicated to the brain by the system of nerves, acting much as a telegraph wire acts, which inform the
brain of the existence of local trouble or distress in
some part of the body. Such perturbations of the
brain, when they occur during sleep, occasion our
dreams; but the lecturer went no further and would
allow no other explanation of the mystery of dreaming than the purely bodily one. There entered into
his definition of dreams nothing that could throw
any light upon the working of the imagination, the
memory, or any of the other faculties of the mind in
sleep—he did not, it would seem, even see how much
his explanation left unexplained. Scientific thought
has moved very far from this standpoint. Some of
the great physicians are devoting themselves to
special branches of medical psychology; they have
come to realise the immense, the almost incalculable,
power of the human mind over the body, and are
therefore ready to study every manifestation of the
mind and its subtle processes; and a wise physician
writing to-day tells us frankly that the medicine of
the future will have to take ever fuller and fuller
account of aspects of human nature which the medi-

cine of yesterday would have dismissed as mere
emotionalism and as wholly outside its province.   If
it is true, as M. Bergson believes, "that the principal
task of psychology in this century will be to explore
the secret depths of the unconscious, and that in this
science discoveries will be made rivalling in importance the discoveries made in the preceding century
in the physical and natural sciences," then it is probable that the observations of each one of us, useless
as these would be if they simply remained individual
notes, may have a real value when they form part
of the accumulating sum of the recorded facts of
man's experience, from which science will at last be
able to formulate laws that are at present unknown.

We may need for this purpose a "Clearing House
of Dreams," where there may be collected the experiences of many men and women trained to record
as accurately as possible their observations of
dreams and of other subtle processes of the mind
and of the subconscious mind.   If science is ever to
make real progress in understanding much that is
now inexplicable with regard to these uncharted
regions, it must be furnished with ample materials,
and materials drawn from widely different sources
and embodying the experiences of very many people.
It seems important that these records, upon which
science may have eventually to base its conclusions,
should not be drawn exclusively, or even in a large
proportion, from the records of the physician's consulting-room.   Much as we owe to the work of physicians who have faithfully pursued this study,

who have seen in it the possible means of solving some of the hardest problems that a doctor has to meet, and who carry forward the science of mind-healing hand in hand with that of the healing of the body, yet the physician starts at a disadvantage in the study of dreams or of other little-understood mental processes. He will be able, no doubt, in his consulting-room to get together a number of relevant and interesting facts, but it is likely that far too small a proportion of his observations will be derived from the experiences of perfectly healthy and normal men and women. "They that are whole have no need of the physician, but they that are sick." The mental processes of those that are whole, the dream imagery of those of us who are fortunate enough to enjoy the soundest bodily and mental health, are much less likely to come under the doctor's notice than are the experiences of nervous or morbid people, or of persons who, owing to temporary conditions of illness, are not for the moment normal or healthy.

This is an almost inevitable drawback to the conclusions that the specialist particularly interested in this study draws from the cases that come under his observation. Almost of necessity his conclusions are influenced by the proportion of more or less morbid subjects that he will come across. This would seem to be explanatory of much that we find in the writings of so great a specialist as Freud. His books have a world-wide reputation, and on them a great school of teaching is based. Freud's dream theory, very briefly stated, is that dreams are deeply significant, but never by any chance significant of what they would appear superficially to mean. They are symbols, he teaches, of desires, thoughts, or fears, that are sternly repressed by day and that are not admitted to our waking consciousness. By day they are therefore unable to intrude their presence upon us, but by night, when our will-power is in abeyance, they come forth unchecked, repeating themselves allegorically and always under a disguise in dreams. He sees in sex impulse the origin and motive power that excites almost all dream thought and action, and in his interpretation of dream symbols he goes so far as to state in all seriousness that dreams which are conspicuously innocent invariably embody erotic wishes. Dr. Freud has so elaborated his theory of the dream as the symbol of repressed desire, and of the distortion of the unconscious wish in the dream figure, that it would seem as if the theory had become an obsession to which the facts have had at times to accommodate themselves. Leaving out of account all the other powerful desires and impulses that actuate our waking lives, he sees sex impulse alone amongst them as the force which is able to affect the dream mind.

The examples that he gives of dreams, of various mental processes, of curious lapses of memory, and of humour in dreams, when not drawn from personal experience, were drawn from the patients of his clinic, from persons, that is to say, who were suffering from every kind of nervous and mental disorder, and this no doubt accounts for their abnormal nature and for their ugliness.

The applications of his theory, as Freud has elaborated it, are unsatisfactory to many of his scientific critics, who have condemned the crudities and exaggerations that they discover in them. The value of Freud's contribution to science would seem to lie, not in these applications to his teaching, or in the deductions that his disciples have drawn from it, but in the new and original point of view which he opened up, and in the great stimulus that he gave to explorers in the field of psychological research.

The principles laid down by Freud have profoundly altered the conceptions of this generation. They have been so unhesitatingly accepted that anyone who should question their universal applicability would find himself in a small minority, for the modern school of psycho-analysis that is based on Freud's teaching has an immense vogue both in this country and in America. A study of the numerous books on the subject available to the ordinary reader has made me feel that a greater measure of critical common sense might with advantage be brought to bear on the conclusions of some of these writers. I have no wish to make an attack on the new school of teaching; it has the support of great names, and in many cases of nervous disorder the therapeutic value of psycho-analysis has been established. I only venture to question the universal truth of these theories when applied to the dreams of perfectly normal individuals, for my mind remains uncon-

vinced by the explanations and the analyses that are
given of ordinary dreams by Freudian psycho-
analysts. I do not believe that all dreams are
fashioned after the same manner, I am sure that they
differ from one another as widely as our thoughts
differ; and that while some may have their origin
in obscure places of the unconscious, and may be
symbolic of thoughts which are repressed by day, as
Freud teaches, the majority of dreams of sane people
have in all probability a simpler and happier parent-
age.[1] Many of our dreams are indeed symbolic or
allegorical in form, but I believe that they represent
in different ways the moods and thoughts which
have occupied our minds by day. Happily there is
no need for us to believe that the nature of the
dreams which for so many of us make up so great
an element of pleasure in life has any close relationship with the morbid obsessions of disease. Nightmares and dreams of fear exist, other ugly and evil
imaginings may also be hidden away out of sight,
and all these conceptions, side by side with our un-
counted half-forgotten memories of fair and happy
things, are set free when the will that controls them
is wholly or partially suspended at night. But I
believe that not only are these sinister visions and
interpretations exaggerated, but I shall also hope
in this book to show that, in sleep, we are not, or need
never be, left at their mercy, because we can if we
choose exercise a real and effective control over the
nature of our dreams. A sound instinct tells us, and

[1] See Chapter VII, "Symbolism in Dreams."

tells us convincingly, that neither the mind as it works by day, nor that which operates in our dreams, acts after the manner described by some of these writers.

The Freudian theory of dream construction may be true and may be required to explain certain aspects of the dream life of those who are mentally disordered, but I find it very difficult to trace its connection with a dream life that is so profoundly different, or with the working of a dream mind which carries on its activities in close and harmonious co-operation with the normal life of the mind by day.

It is natural that a large proportion of the literature concerning sleep and dreams should be written from the point of view of medical science. The growth of the belief in the therapeutic value of the study of the unconscious has brought this about.

Apart from the numerous school of writers who follow more or less on the lines of Freudian psychoanalysis, the clinical study of dreams has been pursued zealously in France and in America, as well as in this country; and the unprofessional student can only look with respect and some natural awe at the vast library of books that contain the result of these investigations.

Amongst a rarer class of books, those concerned with problems of normal dreaming, with the dreams of sane and healthy persons, Mr. Havelock Ellis's "World of Dreams" seems one of the wisest and most lucid. It is, he says, "by learning to observe and to understand the ordinary nightly experience of dream life that we shall best be laying the foundation of future superstructures. For, rightly understood, dreams may furnish us with clues to the whole of life." [1]

The plea that this study should not be confined to medical science, and that others besides physicians should investigate it from a different standpoint from theirs, is beginning to have a response; and philosophers are occupied to-day with the problem of dreams. M. Bergson, in a lecture delivered originally before the *Institut Psychologique,* and now republished in England, has given us his explanation of the source from which they spring. He does not dwell upon the Freudian theories of repressed desires and symbolic meanings; but he gives us his explanation of dream consciousness and of the method by which he believes that dreams originate. Sensations of sudden light, sensations of sound and of feeling, "which are presented to our eyes, to our ears, to our touch during sleep as well as during waking," make, he tells us, the starting-point of dreams, for our senses remain active, and our faculty of sense impression does not stop whilst we are asleep, although the impressions that are conveyed to our mind are confused and vague. These impressions are, he says, the "raw material out of which memory weaves the web of our dreams." A dream may, for instance, have for its starting-point the sensation caused by a light falling on the face of the sleeper. In the dream this may be con-

[1] Havelock Ellis, "The World of Dreams."

verted into the gleam of moonlight on a pool, into a woman's white dress, or the shining of fire; and similarly a sound which strikes upon the ear whilst we sleep may turn into the thunder of cannon, the roar of a train or the crash of waves breaking on a cliff. The dream imagination has seized upon the sense impression and interpreted it as it pleased, and the dream is forthwith started on its course. The vague indistinct impression that the dreamer received from his eyes, his ears, or sense of touch are caught and are converted into precise and determined objects by his imagination.

In this explanation of the starting-point of dreams in sense impressions, M. Bergson follows closely in the steps of other writers, and especially in those of M. Maury, a French writer who wrote on dreams some forty years ago. M. Maury's theory does not in point of fact carry us very far towards a complete understanding of the problems connected with the working of the mind in sleep. Some dreams certainly have their origin in perturbations of the brain caused by vibrations started from outside the body and striking on the senses; whilst others are started by vibrations proceeding from within the body and communicated by the nerve system to the brain. But it is clear that neither of these statements gives more than a small part of the truth concerning the origin of dreams. They may, indeed, be started by vibrations, just as a thought may be started in that way, but dreams are without doubt also set in motion by the mechanism of the mind and of its faculty memory—just as our thoughts are; and our dreams, like our thoughts, are shaped by the operation of the mind.

Dreams that have their origin in a physical impression are defined by some writers as sensorial dreams, and those that originate mainly in mental impressions and memories as psychic dreams; but this classification needs considerable qualification. It is, of course, no easy matter to trace back a dream to the sense impression which may have started it; because, as such impressions necessarily occur whilst we are asleep, no proof of them is generally available beyond the dream itself.[1] I am convinced that the greater number of my own dreams, especially the long coherent dreams, which are the dreams of my deepest sleep, would come under the heading of psychic dreams; for they evidently have their origin in some strong mental impression, and I find that I am hardly ever aware of the sense impressions which have possibly helped to stimulate them. The mental impressions which start a dream on its course are generally easily recognised, and are in many instances created by emotions or thoughts that have preoccupied the mind during the day. When, however, it happens that the thoughts of our waking hours are thus carried on into our sleep, M. Bergson would have us believe that we are only imperfectly asleep—hardly, he thinks, asleep at all. To use his own words in defining his theory of "disinterestedness"· To sleep is to become disinterested; one

1 Cf. Chapter X.

sleeps to the exact extent to which one "becomes disinterested." And again he says: "*At a given* moment, I become *disinterested* in the present situation, in the present action—in short, in all which previously has fixed and guided my memory; in other words, I am asleep.

"A mother who sleeps by the side of her child will not stir at the sound of thunder, but the sigh of the child will wake her. Does she really sleep in regard to her child? We do not sleep in regard to what continues to interest us."

It is difficult and unwise to dogmatise about such a point as this, as each of us can speak only from his own limited experience; but judging from my own dream experience I should venture to say that this statement of M. Bergson's is not a convincing statement about dreaming sleep. It seems to me a misuse of words to say that we do not really "sleep" unless we cease wholly to be "interested," for the dreams which most often embody the preoccupations of the day are, I find, the deep dreams of the soundest sleeping time, the dreams, that is to say, of the deep night sleep occurring between midnight and about four o'clock in the morning.

The things which have principally absorbed us by day are not, of course, necessarily the things that will occupy the dream mind; but very often they do so occupy it. It happens constantly that some idea that fills our thoughts on one day will determine the course of our dreams either on the following night or, after an interval, a few nights later. For a long time

I have very carefully recorded my dreams, and I find that the greater number of them are clearly suggested or modified by whatever has been the dominant thought or chief interest at the time. For instance, in my records of the dreams of deep sleep during the period from August to December, 1914, and also in 1915, 1916 and 1917, I find that a very large proportion of them were founded on or were modified by the war, which was the natural preoccupation of all minds during those months and years. The anxieties that it involved, the local activities connected with the war, the organisation for the housing and care of war refugees—these thoughts seem to have suggested the greater number of my dreams, or to have worked their way into their fabric.

I did not, in short, to use M. Bergson's phrase, become "disinterested" when I slept; or really "sleep" at all. And yet unless the word is used in some very different sense from the ordinary one, this is certainly not true, for my sleep was deep and real. I know that this constant continuance of interest, this carrying of the thought of the day into the dream life, is not an invariable experience. An artist whose life is one of great absorption in his work tells me that very seldom do the problems of his craft or the thought of his pictures enter into his dreams, even when they completely fill all his waking thoughts. Some authors say that when greatly preoccupied with the books that they were writing they have seldom dreamed of these. The experience of other writers is exactly the reverse of this; their books fill their dreams or make, at any rate, the starting-point from which most of them spring.

Besides dreams which arise from the predominant thought of the day, there are others which have their origin in any book that we are reading, especially if it be read late at night. The tenor of the book will probably be greatly altered in the dream, for the dream mind will seize upon some problem suggested in its pages and will work it out afresh after its own manner. It may, for instance, take the outline of a story, transforming it completely, and evoking something so different from the original that it is hardly to be recognised.

Other dreams there are which grow out of some remembered word or name—a place-name very often. A name which he may have almost forgotten by day starts into prominence when the control of the normal mind ceases. Such a name or word is often the point of crystallisation from which a dream of adventure will radiate. In such a dream each fresh incident that occurs suggests another, and this in turn suggests some other associated idea or fragment of memory. All these float up from the reserves where thousands of remote, half-forgotten impressions must be stored away. The dream mind connects them all together and strings them into a whole, elaborating each incident and each memory in turn. Our intelligence, which, as M. Bergson says truly, does not surrender its reasoning faculty during sleep, insists all the time on finding explanations for every apparent discrepancy, bridging over the gaps, supplying the missing places in the dream story by calling up other memories. So well, indeed, does the reasoning faculty carry out its work, that I find as a rule little of that incongruity and inconsequence in my dreams, that "anarchy" of "dreaming sleep" that de Quincey speaks of and that many writers describe as being so essential a feature of dreaming. On the contrary, the dream imagination and reasoning faculty generally fill up the gaps so effectually that the sequence of ideas and events goes forward quite naturally and without a hitch and with few of the absurdities that people lay so much stress upon.

The fact is there are dreams and dreams, and we must get rid of the assumption that each dream resembles all the others. To class them all together into one or two categories is nearly as absurd as to do the same thing with regard to thoughts, each dream being an intensely individual operation of the mind; so that whilst some pass through strange and confused transformations, many others are as logical and consecutive as an ordinary history of travel or adventure. Mr. Greenwood wrote of his own experience in terms that exactly describe such dreams:

"If there are wildly extravagant dreams without sense or order, others take a course as natural and consistent as an episode in real life. The theory that dreams are always occasioned by mental disorder seems to require that they should always be disorderly too, but they are not. Many are not. I cannot suppose that my experience differs from thousands of others; and not rarely, but commonly, I have dreams which are throughout as consistent in scene and circumstance as any story. Sometimes they are romantic and surprising; but none the less they move from point to point on a perfectly rational course. The little drama proceeds quite naturally, with no incursions of the grotesque, no lapse into extravagance, but often with slight Defoe-touches; such as the novelist thinks himself happy in contriving to heighten the similitude of his story   Contrivance is the word that would most certainly apply to the whole structure of such dreams were they the written work of the working day. . . . Another noteworthy characteristic of these dreams is that they seem to tale easily from a store of invention distinct from that which we draw upon with more or less effort in our waking hours." "My dreams," he adds elsewhere, "are almost invariably as pleasant as reading in a good book of romance, or listening to strange significant stories of real life."[1]

I could not claim that all my own dreams have the adventurous and imaginative quality of the dreams described by Mr. Greenwood. Some happily have these qualities, just as some days in our life also possess them, days when a fine sense of adventure seems to be in the very air we breathe; but there are many other more "every-day" dreams that lack these romantic qualities but which are nevertheless the

[1] Frederick Greenwood, "Imagination in Dreams," a book which, though written many years ago, still seems to me one of the most enlightening of all the studies of dreams, and for the unprofessioual student a most suggestive introduction to the subject.

source of great enjoyment; giving the same kind of
quiet pleasure that we feel when journeying through
an unfamiliar country, when each little hill we sur-
mount and each bend of the road that we turn reveals
to us something new, and the attention is held absorbed by all the simple incidents and homely beau-
ties of the wayside. Just so do some dreams make
their quiet and pleasant progress. Tranquil as they
are, they have all the charm of the unexpected, the
unfamiliar. The incidents of some such dreams written down next morning might seem almost too simple
to record, but so also would the incidents of many
days of happy travel. A curious sense of pleasure
and well-being seems to pervade them that is out of
all proportion to the incidents that happen in their
course. In coherent dreams such as these the reasoning faculty, the memory, and the imagination are
all called upon to bear a part, after the same fashion,
though not perhaps in the same degree, as when these
faculties are used in the construction of a work of
imagination; and the fact that many dreams are of
such a nature shows at least that no mere physiological description of their origin suffices to explain
them wholly to us.

We ask what dreams are—how the dream mind
works which produces them—and our intelligence
refuses to be satisfied with an answer which tells us
merely what physical causes may have started them.
The very nature, the characteristics of such dreams
makes it equally impossible for us to rest content
with theories that see in them only the working of a

mind in disorder, or only the symbolic representations of repressed desire. Neither do we feel that they are explained to us when we are told that functional disturbances set up disturbances of the brain and that these are the cause of our dreams. Even the fact that they may be started by vibrations of sound, of light, or of touch, making sense impressions upon the body, does not carry us very far towards their comprehension.

The physiologist may be able to show us how the beginnings of a dream occur, "but he cannot get beyond a statement of how and where they make their beginning. He does not, and cannot, give us the answer to the question 'What are our dreams?' What faculties of the mind are mostly displayed in them? Which, if any, remain dormant? Does any mental faculty (such as imagination) change its character in our dreams, assume functions of which we are unconscious when awake, or exhibit powers and properties that only appear in sleep? ... In fine, what do our dreams teach us about the constitution of the mind and its potentialities as a whole?" [1]

This, indeed, is the question that we would ask— the thing that we most desire to know. Our task as students of dreams should therefore be to find out by experiment and careful observation all that we can learn about the working of the various mental faculties in the dream state; to find out, for instance, in what way the memory works in sleep, to discover as much as possible about the extraordinary func-

[1] F. Greenwood, "Imagination in Dreams."

tions of the imagination in dreams and the superior
powers and activity that it develops; to study the
operation of the mind in the borderland between
sleeping and waking, and to ascertain whether any
one of our mental faculties is in abeyance whilst we
dream, and if so to what extent does it cease to
work? Is our will-power, for example, totally suspended when we sleep, as many authorities assume
it to be; or is it able, at any rate, to exercise a
partial control over our other faculties? This question of the suspension of the will-power during sleep
is one of special interest; underlying as it does the
whole theory of "disinterestedness" as defined by
M. Bergson. It is a widely held belief that when we
dream the controlling and selecting power of the
mind entirely ceases. But does it actually cease? I
believe that it is not necessarily suspended, and
that if we choose we can still exercise a considerable degree of selection and control over our
dreams.

It is a matter of common experience that we can
wake up at will at a given hour that has been resolved
on overnight; the will in that case operates to awaken
the sleeper at a definite moment, and it cannot, therefore, have been in a state of entire suspension. I
have found also that by adopting certain methods
and by acquiring a certain discipline of mind we can
ensure that our will shall retain a very considerable
degree of influence over our dream mind, an influence
sufficient to give us a real and effective measure of
command over our dreams.

This point has long been one of especial interest to me, and the notes that are given in the next chapter on the subject of dream control, slight and inconclusive as they may be, embody observations that have been made during a period of many years.

CHAPTER II

DREAM CONTROL

If there were dreams to sell,
What would you buy?
Some cost a passing bell,
Some a light sigh,
That shakes from Life's fresh crown
Only a rose-leaf down.
If there were dreams to sell,
Merry and sad to tell,
And the crier rung the bell,
What would you buy?
                    —Thomas Beddoes, *Dream Pedlary.*

"If there were dreams to sell," if indeed the dream-pedlar could bring us the dreams of our desire, how well we know what we would choose; the faces that we would summon in our sleep, the paths that our feet should tread, the familiar rooms known to us long ago, in which we would find ourselves again—if we could buy. Is there any key that will open the doors of dreaming at our will? Any secret which would give us the power of choice or control over the activities of our sleeping hours? Elusive phantom-like things our dreams are, evading the memory which would hold them fast, refusing often to come at our bidding, however great our longing may be; but although this is true, and although we may never find any magic word of power that will give us perfect mastery over them, yet I am sure that there are some simple secrets, some methods that can be learned, by means of which we may in some measure command them, and that, more than we yet realise, the control of our dreams lies within our power.

We shall only be able to enjoy the full value of our heritage in the dream world when we have discovered how to make full use of our powers of happy dreaming, and have learned to exercise at any rate a certain amount of selection and of control over the nature of our dreams. It is obvious that the advantages of such control would be great, but it will probably be objected that it is impossible radically to alter their character, and that the elimination of unhappy or evil dreams, and the cultivation of pleasurable dreaming are equally outside our powers. The mind in sleep, it is often alleged, will always remain independent of our waking thoughts. A philosopher as wise as M. Bergson assumes this to be the case, and bases his dream theories on the assumption; but a long personal experience teaches me that the dream mind is far less independent of our will than is supposed, and that, to a degree that is not generally thought possible, the waking mind can and does direct the activities of the mind in sleep. I believe, in short, that we can at will stop the recurrence of ''bad'' dreams, or of dreams that we dislike or dread, and that we can, to a considerable extent, alter the very nature of our dreams by using in our sleep the same faculty of rational selection and rejection that we use with regard to our thoughts and to our wandering fancies by day. We shall find, when the habit is learned, that we can make desired dreams recur more or less at will, and that we can develop in them certain qualities and powers. In this way the habit of dream control will gradually become ours. That we should be able to acquire such power should not, indeed, seem surprising, for much of the latest teaching of science points in the same direction, and offers possible clues to the meaning of experiences that are familiar to some of us who are students of dreams. If we may provisionally accept as a working hypothesis the theory that "every human organism comprises two mental selves or personalities, the normal one and one that comes into activity only under hypnosis or in our dreams," [1] this may actually give us such a clue, and help to solve some of the difficulties that present themselves. Every day more is being ascertained about the power of "suggestion" that one mind can exercise over another. It is proved by well-attested experiments that, under the influence of hypnotic suggestion, control, not only of the mind, but of the organic processes of the body, can be established, and that the power of memory and the powers of the senses can be controlled and even greatly heightened in this condition. If by means of suggestion one mind can thus control another, can command its obedience, and actually exalt its powers of memory and imagination, it should not be impossible to con-

[1] W. McDougal, *Encyclopædia Britannica*, "Hypnotism."

ceive of a process by which our normal consciousness is able to control to some degree the working of our subconscious or dream mind in sleep. Parallel and very similar to this process is the control that we all, consciously or unconsciously, exercise over what are popularly called our "nerves" and over the organic processes of our own bodies. The lessons learned by all who have acquired disciplined habits of mind and body suggest that there is nothing fundamentally improbable in the belief that we should be able to control the actions and the imagination of the subconscious self in dreams. The problem is how to acquire this controlling power, how, in short, we are to set up in the dream mind such a habit of response and obedience to the command of the waking mind as to make voluntary dreaming possible.

Much may have been written on this subject that I have not yet discovered. I have not found in books much to help me in gaining this power, nor many records of other persons who have sought for or have acquired it. Mr. Frederick Myers gave a few instances of such experiments, and no doubt there are others who have found out more than I have done, and who have advanced further on these lines. Perhaps each of us has at present to puzzle out a solution of our own. Each student of dreams who tries to get some measure of dream control can only record his own limited personal experience; the sum of all such experiences might be of great future value were there a clearing house of dreams; but as this does not yet exist, I can only write of my own limited and partially successful experiments in dream control—first in eliminating a certain class of dream, and secondly in cultivating a dream that I wanted to recur, by heightening and intensifying its pleasurable elements.

Our first practical needs when we begin to acquire any control over our dreams is to get rid of "bad dreams" of all sorts; for whether they take the form of dreams of grief, dreams of evil, or dreams of fear, "bad dreams" are the occasion of real misery to very many people. Children and grown-up persons often confess that if they had their choice they would rather never dream at all than face the chance of a bad dream or the recurrence of some particular night-fear which they have learned to dread.

Charles Lamb has described the anguish of his own sensitive childhood from this cause. "I was dreadfully alive to nervous terrors. The night-time, solitude, and the dark, were my hell. The sufferings I endured in this nature would justify the expression. I never laid my head on my pillow, I suppose, from the fourth to the seventh or eighth year of my life, without an assurance, which realised its own prophecy, of seeing some frightful spectre."

There are few of us who have not suffered in childhood from dreams which gave us something of the same sense of hopeless and inexplicable terror. It is of no use simply to tell those who suffer in this way that bad dreams are caused by mismanaged digestive or other organic processes, and this is in any case only a very partial explanation of the trouble. It may very likely be true that many dreams have their origin in some bodily discomfort which is communicated to the brain, or they may be suggested by some underlying and perhaps unsuspected physical cause, and in many cases much can be done by finding and following sound rules of bodily health; but it is also a matter of common knowledge that a dream which may have been started originally by some local bodily trouble may go on for a long period of time, repeating itself indefinitely like the repetition of an echo, or like the thousand reflections that are thrown from one mirror to another from opposite walls; so the dream will persist long after its original physical cause is past and forgotten. Our problem is how to rid ourselves effectually of all these disturbing night visions. Aided at first by a chance dream, and later by certain definite methods of thought, I have been able to free myself from all "fear dreams" by one method, and by another method to make "grief dreams" or dreams of distress powerless to disturb me.

A suggestion that greatly helped me to cure such dreams came from an experience that is common to almost every one. Probably we have all at some time or another realised that our dream was "only a dream" and not a waking reality. The idea contained in this very general experience made the point from which I succeeded in starting a successful experiment in dream control. On various occasions long ago, when a dream of grief or terror was becoming intolerably acute, the thought flashed into my sleeping mind, "This is only a dream; if you wake, it will be over, and all will be well again." If only we could ensure the realisation of this fact directly bad dreams appeared, they would cease to have any terrors for us, for a way of escape would always be open. Therefore I tried repeating this formula to myself from time to time, during the day and on going to bed, always in the same words—"Remember this is a dream. You are to dream no longer"— until, I suppose, the suggestion that I wanted to imprint upon the dream mind became more definite and more powerful than the impression of any dream; so that when a dream of distress begins to trouble me, the oft-repeated formula is automatically suggested, and I say at once: "You know this is a dream; you shall dream no longer—you are to wake." For a time after this secret had been fully learned, this would always awaken me at once; nowadays, the formula having been said, I do not have to wake, though I may do so, but the original fear dream always ceases. It is simply "switched off," and a continuation of the dream, but without the disturbing element, takes its place and goes forward without a break.

There is nothing in this very simple method but what any one can carry out for himself if he be so inclined, an occasional steady concentration of the mind upon the formula that is to be used being all that is needed. In practice I find that, whatever form of words is decided upon, it should at first be repeated rather frequently, sometimes aloud, and always in the same words; and as it is easier to most of us to learn prose or poetry by heart, if the thing to be learnt is read over before going to sleep, so, until the formula has become a habit of mind, it should be repeated, if possible, just before we sleep.

In most cases the disordered dream is stopped by a simple word of command, which either ends it abruptly as the falling of the stage curtain brings the play to a close, or which ends it by changing the dream scene, as one magic lantern picture fades out and gives place to another.[1]

The following dream note shows how the formula can be used to get rid of the element of fear in a dream without the necessity of awakening from it:—

During the course of a long dream I had succeeded in tracing the existence of a complicated and dangerous plot against our country. The conspirators had turned upon me on discovering how much I knew. I was so closely followed, and my personal danger became so great, that the formula for breaking off a dream flashed into my mind and automatically gave me back confidence; I remembered that I could make myself safe; but with the feeling of safety I also realised that if I were to wake my valuable knowledge of the dangerous conspiracy would be

[1] A dream which probably haunted and broke the rest of numberless women during the years between 1914 and 1919 was one in which ill news came to us by telegram of husband or of sons at the front. Like other mothers, I suffered anguish from such a dream, until I learnt how to master it by this formula. It would be difficult to express how great was the relief when I knew that I could lie down to sleep free from this particular dread.

lost, for I realised that this was "dream knowledge." It was a dreadful dilemma—safety called me one way, but the conviction that my duty was to stay and frustrate the traitors was very strong. I feared that I should give way, and I knelt and prayed that I might have courage not to seek safety by awakening, but to go on until I had done what was needed. I therefore did not wake; the dream continued. The arch-conspirator, a white-faced man in a bowler hat, had tracked me down to the building where I was concealed, and which by this time was surrounded; but all fear had departed, the comfortable feeling of great heroism, only fully enjoyed by those who feel themselves to be safe, was mine. It became a delightful dream of adventure, since the element of fear had gone from it.

This question of our power of control over our dreams becomes a practical one, and of serious importance, when we realise how closely it touches the health and happiness of our children; for the evil dreams that oppressed Charles Lamb's sensitive childhood are unhappily shared in more or less degree by many children, and are too often the cause of anguish to them. It would be a great gain if those who suffer thus could be helped to understand the nature of their troubles and to become to some extent the masters of their dreams.

It is useless to try to protect the children we love from this particular misery by keeping away from them all impressions that seem to us likely to produce bad dreams; for from the most harmless things in the world, from the picture of a friendly farmyard on the nursery wall, the child's dream imagination will fashion its own fear, and create for itself a thing of horror. We know from Lamb's account how the hated picture of the raising of Samuel gave to his midnight terrors "the shape and manner of their visitation"· " had I never met with the picture, the fears would have come self-pictured in some shape or other. . . . 'Headless bear, black man, or ape' but as it was, my imagination took that form."

Charles Lamb understood only too well how intangible these night-fears of childhood are; how often the dread is spiritual in its nature, "remote from fear of bodily injury to ourselves . . . strong in proportion as it is objectless on earth." And this dread has to be borne alone, since it is generally unconfessed and unshared. A child's silence about his bad dreams adds to the power that they have to make him suffer. He may be willing to speak of his good dreams, but he is often ashamed to say anything about the night-terror that oppresses him. He is checked by the mere possibility that the fears that are so real to him, but that he can hardly put into words, will be met with a smile; and so he does not venture to speak of things that by day he knows will seem absurd, but which nevertheless have power to torture him inexpressibly when night falls. Now if a child is to be helped at all in this matter there must first of all be deeply rooted in his heart an absolute confidence that he will not be laughed at. The child's confidence in his mother about his dreams would be no bad criterion of his trust in her understanding and sympathy. If his confidence has been once gained, how can he be helped to master his night-fears? Many people will say that there is nothing that can be done. I believe, on the contrary, that in the early years of childhood most of us could easily be taught simple methods of control, such as those that I have described, which would be effective in stopping this misery. If a child once knows that he is not defence-less, and that he possesses in his own will-power a real and efficient weapon against his bad dreams, he will assuredly learn how to use it. You give him hope, and you take away from him the paralysing sense of helplessness that is almost the worst part of the trouble.

One of the processes by which this control can be obtained has been described. The form of words to be taught or suggested to a child for its use should, of course, be as short and as simple as possible. It may be, if you will, in some such words as, "This is only a dream—it must stop," or any other similar formula. Whatever words are to be used, they must be repeated very often, especially on going to bed, until they are so familiar that when the bad dream occurs the formula will automatically flash into the dream mind at the same time. In my experience this will soon suffice to put a stop to it. The method of dream control will be most easily imparted to a child in the form of a story about other children and their

dreams.[1] If the theory about dreams is true, which
is described in this book, and on which I have acted
for many years, namely that by thinking about our
dreams we can influence them and can definitely alter
their character, a child's dream life might be greatly
and happily modified in this way. Whatever talents
for delightful dreaming he may possess will be encouraged, and he will learn to enjoy this good gift
without the fear that now too often spoils the antici-
pation of dreaming—the fear of evil dreams. There
are, of course, many other kinds of bad dreams,
apart from these night-fears of childhood and other
"fear dreams." The rest of one sleeper is broken
by vivid imaginings of loss or estrangement, whilst
another describes the strange sense of fathomless
despair that he experiences and dreads. We know
from medieval literature that many dreams used to
be regarded as directly sent by the Enemy of mankind. Dreams of evil and dreams of desire, that
were natural but unlawful to the recluse, no doubt
often assailed the hermit or the inmates of the
cloister, their life of stern repression leaving them
more helplessly at the mercy of such troublous
dreams than others are.[2] In the "Form of Living,"
written by Richard the Hermit for the guidance of

[1] The imaginary children whose dream adventures I should tell
of should not only learn to master their bad dreams by these methods, but they should go on to find out for themselves the pleasures
of dream adventures and travel, and the joy of learning to fly. To
be effective the story should be very simply and prosaically told.

[2] Cf. Chapter XIV.

the Anchoress Margaret, he tells her of "six maners
of dremes (in thus many maners touches the ymage
of dremes men when they slepe.)" Two of these
he tells her, come from over-eating, and "such no
man, holy or other, may escape." The third comes
from "Illusions of the Enemy," and he warns her
that "where many dremes er, thare er many vanitees,
and many that may make to erre.

We may, happily for ourselves, be free from most
of the uncomfortable dreams that Richard Rolle described, but whatever our particular night-fear or
special dream of grief may be, most people would
agree that a method that would enable us to get rid
of the dreams that we dislike or dread would be an
incalculable boon. The need must be as old as
dreaming itself, and people in all ages have sought
a way by which it could be accomplished.

Amongst a collection of objects lately exhibited in
London, illustrative of superstitions that had survived from a past age and that had lingered on into
this century, there were to be seen certain stones
pierced by natural holes, which were intended to be
hung as a talisman over the bed of sleepers afflicted
with bad dreams. Many such simple charms were
no doubt used; I have not tested the efficacy of any
of these, the only magic or spell that I have personally proved being the formula that I have already
described, and a second formula that I have also
found useful, and that is described in the next chapter.

In making and describing these experiments in

dream control the desirability of getting rid of bad dreams has been assumed; and probably the majority of dreamers would make this assumption and would agree that they would gladly rid themselves of all dreams of distress if they could do so by some simple method. It must, however, be noted that from another point of view—that of the Freudian psycho-analyst—repression or control, leading to the abolition of bad dreams, is no unmixed blessing, but is in all likelihood a mistake. He sees in the bad dream a definite warning, hidden under a symbolical form, of some physical or moral evil, a warning which may only be disregarded at our peril, just as the ordinary symptoms of disease may only be disregarded at grave risk. The effect of controlling the content of our dreams is, he tells us, to force them to hide their true significance, so that the problems which they symbolise are only able to appear under a still more complete disguise: bad dreams are therefore looked on by him as warnings, beneficial if properly interpreted, not as evils to be avoided.

It will perhaps only become possible for us to adopt this attitude, and to welcome, instead of shunning, evil dreams, when we have learned to have a more unquestioning faith in the teachers of the new school of healing who are prepared to furnish us with the interpretation of our dreams; but this faith must first be attained, and until our conviction as to the reliability of their analysis is more assured, there will probably be a majority of people who would gladly make the exchange that I have suggested, and rid themselves of their bad dreams even if these be fraught with possible instruction, in return for a dream life peaceful and unsullied, in which the happier experiences of the day are reflected and the adventures of the imagination are carried on without fear of any ugly or terrifying interruption.

CHAPTER III

I sing the praise of dreams. Daily will I give thanks to the Highest for the freeing of the spirit of man from the labour and sorrows that are his by day. For dreams, the delight of the world, I will give praise.

Besides the formula which was given in the last chapter, which conveys to the dream mind the message that the dream is only a dream which can be altered or ended at our pleasure, there is another which I have also found to be successful in getting rid of dream fears. This method is described in the following notes on flying dreams which are taken from the notes that I have made and kept for many years.

Flying dreams form only one variety of the many happy dreams that have added so much pleasure to my life. I have chosen this class of dreams to speak of more particularly because they furnish the examples that I can most easily quote of the process of dream control, and of the use of a formula in obtaining that control. They show also that by an act of will, and by some concentration of thought upon them, they may be cultivated, with the result that greatly heightened dream powers, such as the perfected faculty of dream flight, may be acquired with-

37

out any serious difficulty, and with great advantage to ourselves.

My first recollections of flying dreams go back to when I was a very little child, when we were living in London. The flying dream, when it first came, was connected with the sensation of fear. Half-way up the dimly lighted staircase that led to our nursery a landing opened on to a conservatory. The conservatory by day was a sunny place full of the pleasantest associations, but with the coming of darkness its character changed altogether. In the night-time anything might be imagined to lurk in its unlighted corners; decidedly it was safest always to hurry past that landing, and even past the other landings which, though they did not open on to any such dark spots, were not places where a child cared to linger alone. In some of the first dreams that I can remember I was on that staircase, fearful of something which I was especially anxious never to have to see. It was then that the blessed discovery was made, and that I found that it was just as easy to fly downstairs as to walk; that directly my feet left the ground the fear ceased—I was quite safe; and this discovery has altered the nature of my dreams ever since. At first I only flew down one particular flight of steps, and always downwards; but very soon I began to fly more actively. If anything began to alarm me in my dreams, I used to try to rise in the air, but for some years I was unable to rise to any great height, or to fly with real ease. It was only gradually that the flying dream ceased to be connected with the sensation of fear and escape. For a long time it was often an effort to fly; every year, however, made it easier and more sure. By degrees "bad dreams" left me. When once I realised that I could always escape by flight, the sense of the something unknown, to be escaped from, became a thing of the past; but the power of flying grew and has steadily improved all my life.

The actual process by which I fly in my dreams has always been the same since the earliest days when I first fluttered down the nursery staircase. From what others have told me, there seems to be a good deal of variety in the manner in which different people fly. By giving a slight push or spring with my feet I leave the ground and fly without further effort, by a simple act of volition. A slight paddling motion by my hands increases the pace of the flight, and is used either to enable me to reach a greater height, or else for the purpose of steering, especially through any narrow place, such as through a doorway or window. If I am at all fatigued by a long flight, this motion of the hands is of great assistance and gives confidence and increased power.

Differing slightly from the flying dream is the gliding dream, which is also a very common and widely shared experience. In this dream the feet are not used and do not move at all; I glide a few inches above the ground, as though I were walking in the ordinary way, but without any effort.

Flying or gliding dreams, in whatever shape they occur, bring with them a keen sense of pleasure.

Even when such a dream is full of varied incident or
adventure, it is always restful and refreshing.   I
awake reluctantly from it with a sense of regret that
it should be over.   Its outlines are generally very
clear-cut and easily recalled to memory, and it is
hardly ever inconsequent, as some dreams are.   I
have no doubt that the increased power of flight
which I now enjoy, and which has been a matter of
steady growth, is to be attributed to the system that
I have described.   Thinking about these dreams has
certainly enabled me to dream them.   When I had
discovered the method by which bad dreams could be
got rid of, I tried to find out how far I could consciously control dreaming by inducing a particular
dream to recur.   I found that if I steadily thought
about such a dream as the flying dream it would soon
come back.   It will not, indeed, come exactly to order,
but it will come after a short interval.   I have never
been able exactly to measure this interval; it may be
of two or three nights, or it may be longer, varying
very much according to the definiteness with which
the waking mind has been concentrated upon the
idea.   Especially after talking about flying I find
that I am certain very soon to dream of it.

I have tried also to see how far, by thinking of the
dream, I could accomplish some definite result in it;
how far, for instance, I could perform some new and
difficult act of flight.   It was a long time before I
could fly higher than five or six feet from the ground,
and it was only after watching and thinking about
the flight of birds, the soaring of the larks above the

Wiltshire Downs, the hovering of a kestrel, the action of the rooks' strong wings, and the glancing flights of swallows, that I began to achieve in my dreams some of the same bird-like flights. After I had thought long and often about flying over high trees and buildings, I found that I was getting the power to rise to these heights with ever lessening difficulty and effort.

I then became anxious above all things to achieve a dream in which I should fly over the sea. The dream came at last, and I found myself on the shore looking at the waters of the Atlantic. Beginning at first with short uncertain flights over the sea, I soon found that I need not fear. Flying in the air or gliding on the water was equally safe and easy, and so I started, and with a flight like that of a sea-gull, I flew away with boldness across the Atlantic waves.

The motions of aeroplanes have of late years suggested similar dreams, in which I take the pilot's place, and steer a small aeroplane through the looping flights of the practised airman. Mechanical difficulties are rare in dreams of flying, and if anything untoward does happen (and even in my dreams I do not understand an engine) I have only to desert my plane and to take refuge in my natural way of flight.

A dream that I recorded many years ago gave me a second formula which has been of use to me ever since. By giving confidence in my power to fly it has not only been the source of great pleasure by making difficult experiments in flying easy, but it has given a greatly increased sense of security from all bad dreams. Fear may come into a dream, but this need not trouble us if, by a bird's flight, the dreamer can quickly be carried into safety; for confidence in one's power of flight will then be all that is needed.

In my dream I was present at a party given in the rooms of the Royal Society in Burlington House. Lord Kelvin, Lord Rayleigh, Sir William Ramsay, my brother-in-law, Sir Arthur Rucker, and many others whom I knew, were there. They were standing together in a little group, and my brother-in-law asked me to explain to them my method of flying. I could not explain how it was done, only that it seemed to me much easier to fly than to walk. At his suggestion I made some experimental flights—circling round the ceiling, rising and falling, and showing them also the gliding or floating movement near the ground. They all discussed it critically as though they were rather "on the defensive" about the proceeding, looking upon it, I think, as a new and doubtful experiment, rather savouring of a conjuring trick. Then Lord Kelvin came forward and, speaking with that gracious manner that his friends so well remember, said that he felt the power of human flight to be less surprising, less baffling than the others seemed to think it. "The law of gravitation had probably been in this case temporarily suspended."—"Clearly this law does not for the moment affect you when you fly," he said to me. The others who were present agreed to this, and said that this was probably the solution of the puzzle. An assistant was standing behind the group of men, and in order to show them that flying is not really difficult, I took his hand, and begging him to have confidence in me and to trust to my guidance, I succeeded in making him fly a few inches from the ground.

Since then, when I fly, if people notice the flight at all, which is very seldom, Lord Kelvin's explanation always seems to satisfy them. His reply also gave me the second formula that I can make use of in a dream in case of need, and, like the original formula, it is always successful.

I have sometimes fancied in the middle of a flight that I am losing my power to fly; I have begun then to drift downwards in the air, and have failed to rise again easily. At such moments the "word of power" comes into my mind, and I repeat to myself, "You know that the law of gravitation has no power over you here. If the law is suspended, you can fly at will. Have confidence in yourself, and you need not fear." Confidence is the one essential for successful flight, and confidence being thus restored, I find that I can fly again with ease.

It seems to be a matter of common experience that partial failure of power in a dream generally occurs when the dreamer is emerging from the deepest levels of sleep and is approaching the waking level. In very deep sleep all sense and remembrance of our tired body and relaxed limbs disappear, and we are therefore able to carry on every dream movement with ease. It is only when we come nearer to the moment of awakening that consciousness of our physical condition begins to interfere with the dream imagination and that a sense of effort comes in.

This question of effort or inhibition of movement in dreams is fully discussed in various books. Mr. Havelock Ellis gives a very interesting description of it and of its probable causes. He says: "When in dreams we become conscious of difficult movement, it has frequently, and perhaps usually, happened that the motor channels are not entirely closed, the sensory channels unusually open, and very frequently, though not necessarily, this is associated with the approach of awakening. . . . The question of movement in dreams, of the presence or absence of effort and inhibition, is explicable by reference to the depth of sleep and the particular groups of centres involved. The full normal sleep movements are purely ideatory, and no difficulty arises in executing any movement, for the reason that there is no movement at all, or even any attempt at movement. Movement or attempt at movement tends to occur when the motor and sensory centres are in a partially aroused state; it is a phenomenon which belongs to the period immediately before awakening." [1]

People who suffer from nightmares describe their total inability to move in the presence of some imminent danger as being the most painful feature of such dreams. I have not actually experienced this kind of dream, but it has often happened in the course of a long flight that I have found my powers of

[1] Havelock Ellis, "The World of Dreams."

flying gradually lessening and to some extent failing me.

Formerly this loss of power used to herald my awaking from the dream, but now I either use the "formula" which gives confidence and restores the power to fly or the memory of previous experiences comes to my aid, and I recollect at such moments that by ascending to a slight elevation of any kind, to a hill or the upper story of a building, a fresh start can be made, and I can fly again from this height with renewed vigour. In such a case I do not have to awake; the dream simply takes on a fresh lease of life, and the dream journey or adventures are continued without interruption. The following is an example of such a dream:

November, 1914.

A Flying Dream in War-time

When the dream began I was waiting in a high office-like room which I knew to be closely connected with the War Office. Its walls were painted a light green colour, and whilst I waited I noticed that the prints which hung round it were arranged very irregularly and very high up on the walls. I was expecting a dispatch that I had volunteered to carry to the Army Headquarters in Belgium, flying in the manner in which I fly in my dreams.

There was some delay in its coming, and I flew up round the room partly to test my power of flight, but also to see if the window would make a good starting-place. Whilst I circled round I examined the pictures—one, a small engraving of the second Earl Grey, was framed in a narrow "early Victorian" gold frame, and as it hung crookedly, it caught my attention, and I tried to straighten it, but the nail on which it hung was loose and the picture came off into my hand. At that moment the door opened and an official came in. I descended and began to apologise and explain, but he smiled and said it did not signify. "In fact," he said, "it is rather a lucky coincidence—we were wondering what we could possibly send with you to serve as an introduction or passport. Lord Grey's relationship to Sir Edward Grey, our Secretary of State, is well known abroad. His picture will introduce you at once and be a guarantee of your good faith; you must take it with you!" "How tiresome of the War Office!" I thought; "fancy having to carry this framed picture on my flight!" However, I could not well refuse, and I fastened it as well as I could by means of its cord to my waist. I asked for a map of the country as being absolutely necessary to guide my flight. The official said that they had hunted all over the War Office for a map of Belgium but could only find a very old one; but he added: "This will matter less because all the towns and villages of Belgium are so old that you will find them all marked upon this old map." The map produced was inded very ancient; it was on yellowish paper or parchment, beautifully written, with the names of Flemish towns and villages in old-fashioned characters, but with no railways marked on it and but very few roads. I protested, but it was all I could get. "You will fly over Naville and . . . and Dischemoote," I was told. I wondered anxiously how I should recognise all these places as I flew over them, but I need not have troubled about this. I found afterwards that it was not so difficult as I had imagined, for the country itself, as seen from above, looked singularly like the map.

It was getting dark now, and I was to start when it was dark enough for me to be practically unseen. I flew up to the window, and holding my awkward map before me, I stood on the ledge and flew out over the roofs of a foreign-looking town. I saw below me first of all houses and streets, then a road which passed through various scattered houses and villages. "There is Naville," I thought. . . . I flew on and on, and presently began to get tired. I was flying rather low by now, and this made me anxious, for it was beginning to get lighter, and I could see groups of men standing about in the dim light— they were dressed in odd, dark-brown clothes (like Dutchmen I thought). I was not afraid of them, but I knew that I must get away if I were to take my dispatch safely to its destination. Once I nearly descended amongst them, but I got away in time, and unseen, and entered a house. I ran up its staircase and found my way to an upper window, from which I flew off at a good height from the ground and with a strong steady flight. The sky was getting lighter, and I saw against the dawn a

row of ragged wind-swept trees.   There were many
other incidents by the way which I forget; but at
last I arrived at my destination—the Army Headquarters.   The place was a strange castle. . . . I
entered with the War Office dispatch and found in
supreme command there Mr. Winston Churchill, to
whom I gave the paper and from whom I had to receive my instructions.   I was escorted through the
castle passages to where, underground, beneath the
castle itself, in strange vaulted halls, a royal court
was installed.   A stately procession, a king, a queen
and attendants, were passing down a high arched
corridor of this underground palace into which I
looked.   Although it was broad daylight above, the
halls were lighted artificially and the atmosphere
of the whole place seemed curious and unnatural,
and a longing came over me to leave the castle as I
had come to it, by flight.

No one stopped me, and I followed a boy in
Scout's uniform up to the open air into the court-
yard, where a party of Belgian Boy Scouts were
practising experiments in flying and were achieving
short, spasmodic flights under the direction of Mr.
Winston Churchill.   Their funny attitudes amused
me, and I stood laughing and watching—"They
look like frogs trying to fly," I thought.   I passed
on, and made my way up to the great outer walls
of the castle, and I then saw how shattered and
ruined its ramparts were.   The narrow walk leading round the top of the walls was broken away in
places and was very dangerous, but the gaps in the

path did not trouble me, for where walking is dangerous flying is safe, and from these walls I started afresh and flew away.

.   .   .   .

Oftenest of all nowadays the flying dream occurs in surroundings of lofty rooms and the great staircases of palatial buildings which I do not know. Sometimes I am in the British Museum or one of the other public galleries. I want to get to the end of the long rooms, and I fly lightly along them. As a bird in a room naturally flies along the ceiling, I float upwards and fly along at that level. One does not realise, until one gets accustomed to flying instead of walking, how big a space there is between the ceiling and the tops of doors and windows. One has to float downwards for some distance and steer through the doorway in order to get from room to room or from one gallery to another. When the flying or gliding dream begins I find myself always now in my "flying dress"—it is a dress of straight close folds which fall three or four inches below my feet. The reason for this is that, once or twice when I have been moving among crowds in busy streets, gliding just clear of the ground, I thought that people must notice that my feet never move like theirs. In Oxford Street one day, when the pavement was very crowded, I feared that it would attract attention disagreeably if people noticed this fact, and that the curiosity of it might lead to an inconvenient amount of notice. I left the thronged thoroughfare and went quickly down Duke Street to avoid observation. Once in the quieter street, I flew along comfortably, but the next time I began to dream I found that I wore a long dress which hid my feet entirely, and no one can now see that I am not walking just as they are. It has struck me sometimes as a curious thing that, however crowded the rooms may be when I am flying, no notice whatever is taken even of the most daring flights, but I have learnt now that this is almost always the case. Either it is quite unnoticed or more probably I am unseen.

It will be seen from these extracts from my notes on flying dreams that beyond the power of eliminating or ending bad dreams, which has been a great gain, the measure of control that I have been able to acquire is limited, amounting to a certain power of making a favourite dream recur more or less at will, and of being able greatly to increase its pleasurable features. Beyond this I have not gone, and perhaps if our success were greater, if our control were to become more perfect, our pleasure in dreaming would be lessened. If our dreams could be successfully harnessed and brought under even the measure of discipline to which our wandering thoughts have to submit by day, they would cease to have the charm which their unexpectedness gives them, and with the loss of freedom they would lose one of their greatest attractions. But we need not fear—nature will take only too good care that our control shall not go too far, and that the spontaneity and freedom of our dreams shall never be too seriously crippled. In making the simple experiments that I have made I have had no idea of bringing my dreams into any strict subjection, but have only tried to ascertain how far will-power really ceases to exercise its functions when we sleep.

To my mind the answer to this question is that it does still exercise considerable authority over the operations of the dream mind, and that its control can, by certain simple methods, and by some concentration of thought, be greatly extended. Memory also, no doubt, takes a part in the causation of such dreams as these. Each dream of flying makes the next flight easier; memories of previous occasions when the dream-consciousness was occupied with these problems tend to act as echoes do and to repeat themselves again and again. And if by day the mind turns from time to time to the same thought and recalls the incidents of some dream adventure, such dreams are apt to reward our remembrance and to come back to us at nightfall at our bidding.

CHAPTER IV

DREAM RECORDING

Yet if little stays with man,
Ah, retain we all we can!
  If the clear impression dies,
  Ah, the dim remembrance prize!
Ere the parting hour go by,
Quick thy tablets, Memory!
  —Matthew Arnold, *A Memory Picture.*

The question of the continuance of activity of
the will during sleep is only one of the many problems that suggest themselves when we begin to
think about the operation of our mental faculties in
the dream state. Equally worthy of note is the
way in which the memory works whilst we sleep, the
way in which it supplies the materials out of which
our dreams are fashioned, calling up from its unseen treasures things new and old, recalling count-
less dimly remembered or forgotten scenes, and impressions that were hardly even sensed by us at
all. Out of these hidden stores memory, aided
by imagination, weaves for us the many-coloured
web of our dreams. But memory has another and
quite different function to perform with regard to
dreams. She not only furnishes us with their
fabric, but she also enables us to recapture and to
record the dream scenes that fade so quickly away

and that are so hard to hold. Hers is the two-fold function of dream-builder and dream-recorder. The part that memory and imagination play in the building of our dreams will be dealt with presently; but meanwhile a brief space must be given here to *dream recording*.

To be able to remember and to write down correctly the sequence of a dream should be an essential qualification for a student of dreams. As a matter of fact, it seems to be a very rare one, and one of the difficulties that faces every one who tries to write seriously about dreams is that of obtaining faithful dream records on which observations can be safely based. If in the future their study is to have any value, it is necessary that we should find out the best methods of making accurate notes of dreams. Anyone who has tried for himself to make such notes, or obtain them from others, will have realised how great this difficulty is, and will have discovered some of the practical obstacles that stand in the way of writing down even a simple dream.

The difficulties are not insuperable, and in this matter of dream recording, as in that of dream control, it is possible, by means of certain easily acquired methods and some concentration of mind, to make accurate notes of dreams if we require to do so. The initial difficulty that meets us is their evanescence; we have all probably experienced the sharp disappointment when we have vainly tried to hold fast the elusive memory of a dream from

which we have just awakened, and have realised
that the more feverishly we strive to remember it
the more intangible it becomes and the more rap-
idly it fades away. Do what we will, we cannot recall more than floating detached fragments, and
glimpses of its scenes. A thick mist of oblivion
seems to come between us and the memory that we
want to recall and literally blots it out. A sea-fog
rolling in over sea and land, and obliterating every
outline, is the best image of the mist of forgetful-
ness that nature often interposes between our
dreams and our waking consciousness. How are
we to roll this back, and recover the scenes and
events that it so quickly hides?

There are, no doubt, many ways that other
dreamers have discovered for themselves. I can
only speak of those that, after long practice, I my
self have found to be successful.

To begin with, the first thought and immediate
occupation of the mind on awaking must be the
recollection of the dream; the only thing further
that is needed is a certain habit of mind that is better expressed in the French word *recueillement*
than in any word of our own. An attitude of quiet
attentiveness should be ours; the mind must be un-
hurried, it must be watchful, as one who looks long
and steadfastly into a still pool to see what is mir-
rored there. As it thus gazes there will come back
to it one by one the scenes of the late dream.

The dream should first be allowed to unroll itself
very quietly *backwards* in a series of slowly moving

pictures, starting from the end and going back through scene after scene to its beginning, until the whole dream has been seen. In order to get a complete record of a long dream, this process should be followed, and then, if possible, the reverse process should be carried out and the dream retraced from its starting-point to its ending. In this way the scenes, events and conversations that have made up the dream story can, when the habit of recollection has been acquired, be retraced. They should then be written down at once. It is only thus, and by making the written notes immediately, that I find it possible to make accurate transcripts of long and complex dreams, and in this fact, no doubt, lies .a great part of our difficulty in getting such records made. The dreamer generally waits until the morning to retrace his dream, and then perhaps tells it or writes it down. It has by that time lost some of its sharp edges and its definition. There will be blank spaces left in his memory; there is nothing easier than for the memory half unconsciously to fill in those blanks. The dreamer may soon begin to think that he remembers what happened in the blurred intervals, or perhaps tries to complete his dream story which broke off with such disappointing suddenness, by an ending that suggests itself, and that makes an artistic finish to the story when it is told the next morning; but as the only possible value of the dream record lies, not in its artistic or dramatic character, but solely in its absolute truthfulness, the dream should always be written down as soon as possible. The mere fact that this is necessary often prevents the dream record being written at all. A "good sleeper" is apt to drop off to sleep again before he has attempted to do it, and an indifferent or "bad sleeper" naturally dreads the complete awakening and probable loss of further sleep if he exerts himself to turn on a light and write down his dream.

There is a real difficulty, moreover, in ensuring that the first action of the mind on awaking from sleep is concentrated on recalling the dream and on nothing else. No other thought must be allowed a foothold until this has been done. To ensure success other ideas must be excluded; for at the moment when the mind is still only half released from the influence of sleep it will naturally turn instantly to whatever has been the preoccupation of the previous day. If we have gone to sleep intent on some specially absorbing thought, that thought, unless kept in check, is sure to come between us and the dream, and to efface the recollection of it, however vivid it may have been. The memory of the clearest dream will not survive for more than a moment the intrusion of such a dominant waking thought; almost instantaneously the dream impression is destroyed. The best way that I know to guard against this, and to make sure of recapturing it, is to determine firmly overnight that nothing shall be allowed to intervene, and that the dream—whatever its nature—shall be recalled directly we wake. The command thus given over-

night will under ordinary circumstances be obeyed
without difficulty, and the dream scenes can be retraced.

There are, however, some conditions which make
it much harder to achieve this success. If the
thought that fills the mind by day is an unusually
absorbing or anxious one, it will actually awaken
us from sleep by its insistence, and then no reso-
lution made over-night will suffice to quell it or to
put it on one side. When we are awakened in this
manner, it may be practically impossible to remember the dream, and its memory will probably elude
us.

Sometimes also when I have tried very vigor-
ously to remember a dream the impression of which
is nebulous, only certain detached floating fragments of it will come back. Dimly I remember
something of it. I have a recollection of skating;
of swift movement on the dark surface of a frozen
river. A recollection of tall trees overhanging the
ice comes back only to fade away again like a "dissolving view," and, in the effort to hold fast the
memory that slips away so quickly, I have fallen
into an error that I find to be always a fatal one if
a dream is to be remembered; I have repeated to
myself in words—not aloud, but mentally—"I was
skating on the frozen river, tall trees were arched
having been conceived in words, instead of seeing
overhead——" but then immediately, the thought
the dream scene as a picture, I see in front of me
the words visualised and written as it were before

my eyes. They may be written in black letters on a white background, or in white letters on a dark ground, but they effectually blot out the dream that I should be watching. The words may next begin to repeat themselves vocally in the ear of the mind as a tune repeats itself and "runs in one's head." Directly the mind vocalises or visualises words in this way they always oust the pictured scenes of the dream, and I know by experience that these are irrevocably lost and that no effort will recapture them.

There are certain classes of dreams which are not easy to record, however soon one may try to write them down. I mean the dreams in which the dreamer passes from one personality into another. Just as a magic lantern picture fades away on the screen and another instantly takes its place, so our actual individuality changes into another, and so also does the individuality of the other actors in the dream. A. starts with me, but B. insensibly takes his place. I may not even know when the change has happened, and though the dream may work out into a coherent and rational story, the dreamer may in the course of it be two or three persons with different histories, characters and associations. The scene and surroundings of the dream may also change in the same fashion: my Wiltshire home fades into the semblance of another house, a house whose threshold I have not crossed for twenty years, and it in turn may give place to the unfamiliar rooms of a strange mansion that I have never seen. How can we retrace and record all these changes? above all when the dream itself shifts, and a second dream, wholy distinct, which I will call the "B" dream, is superimposed on the first; the "B" dream running side by side with the "A" dream. Sometimes the "B" dream is the stronger and takes the place of the other; it is then the one that it is easiest to remember in the morning, but sometimes the "B" dream, after persisting for a time, fades out and the "A" dream may be carried on. Sometimes also, after a very brief waking time, if one falls asleep again, the "B" dream having disappeared, the "A" dream starts afresh from the point where it left off.

It is always very difficult to recall or to describe these changes. In all these cases I think that our notes of dreams must be made very promptly and, except in very clear-cut and well-defined dreams, some blanks must of necessity be left where recollection breaks down or becomes hazy. The following is such a note:

I was sitting in an arm-chair turning over the leaves of a largish book. Its pages were square in shape and showed a wide margin, especially at the top of each page where title headings were printed; the book was printed in very clear black type. I turned over the pages and saw that it contained three stories—"All rather morbid subjects," I thought—and as I read on my dream changed and I became one of the characters in the first story. It was about a husband and a wife and was rather a prosy narrative, but I remember little of the events of it or of the part I played in it, for I thought it dull, and in my capacity as reader I turned over the pages to read the second story.

This was concerned with a murder—a murder that had taken place before the story opened. The man who had committed it was convinced, for reasons that seemed to him wholly adequate, that he was guiltless, and merited no blame for what he had done. I slipped then and there into the person of this man. I remember passionately justifying to myself and to God the righteousness of the act that I had committed. I never felt more certain of anything in my life than I felt then, that my conscience was clear of guilt, and that the dreadful deed that I had done had been right. It was all intensely real to me. I remembered the murderer's haunted journey described in "Oliver Twist." "People who write about a murderer's mind can know very little about it," I thought. Again I turned over a page—"Oh, but these stories are very morbid," I was saying when I woke.

In another of these dreams of changing identity I found myself in the big class-room of a higher elementary school in London. Children were sitting all round me at their desks, and I was a poor child like the rest, newly admitted from a lower grade school, and feeling very forlorn and shy. I thought that they all knew more than I did and had more confidence in themselves. I was sitting unoccupied at my desk, a copy open in front of me, and books. No one had given me directions what to do, and I began to write the "copy," but the letters that I wrote were so badly formed that I felt ashamed, and looked instead into the books. After a time the headmaster came to me and asked how I "had employed the last hour." Alas! I had nothing to show. "Ah!" he said, "that is our little test to see how far you can organise your own work, and use your time." "But you didn't tell me," I said, "and it's my first day." He smiled in a superior way and began to give a lesson to the class. "Where do you all live?" he asked in the course of it. "Hammersmith," said one child, "Chelsea," said another. "Wootton Bassett," said I, and I thought they all smiled. "I am not nearly as grand as they are," I thought. "They are all very superior to me." The class was then summoned to go out, and the headmaster led us for a long walk, taking us, as he said, for an "educational expedition" to see the beautiful old library of one of the Inns of Court.

The ancient room had lately been redecorated with modern wooden panelling, and the master explained in his professional manner, how beautifully it had been done, and at how great a cost. I could see at once that the panelling was rather poor, of the wrong period for the room, and made of indifferent wood. "Does he really think that good?" I asked in a low voice of my neighbour. With this attitude of criticism I ceased to be the school-child and became my own self. I then recognised with a little dismay that the person to whom I had made my whispered criticism was one of the judges of the High Court, who must, it flashed across my mind, probably have been one of those who was responsible, directly or indirectly, for the choice of the panelling. "What a 'gaffe' I have made," I thought; but he was a very charming judge, and he only laughed and said, "It was thought rather good at the time." "But isn't it like the dull decorations inside the House of Commons?" I suggested "Yes," he replied, rather ruefully, "I suppose it is, but I believe we made your husband subscribe to it, for he was a member of this Inn, you know." "I expect you did," I said, and as we sat talking I noticed that the panels in question were really only of deal, but cunningly "grained," so as to look like old oak. The schoolmaster was standing near and, as I felt a distaste for his explanations, and was attracted by the crowd, I wandered away and mingled with the other guests who filled the rooms. I was now wearing a rose-coloured dress of silk that fell in full folds to my feet; it seemed to me beautiful and stately, but very unlike the sheath-like fashionable dresses that other women were wearing. "I haven't worn a rose-coloured dress for years and years," I thought; "no wonder this is old-fashioned, it must have been lying by so long!" "You must come back with us at once," said the schoolmaster, coming up from behind me; and instantly I had turned into the child again in its short, shabby brown frock, hating going back with the other children, hating the long tiresome walk back to school. The Temple Gardens had changed into a wide common, and I skipped round various big clumps of brambles, edging away as far as I could from the master's flow of improving talk. The child's mind was mine again, and mine was the child's rather scornful attitude towards all "grand" attire "I couldn't possibly have skipped like this in that long pink dress," I thought.

I have often written down a dream when I have waked at a very early morning hour. After a while I have slept again, and on re-awakening have found that almost all recollection of the dream that I had previously recorded had so faded that I could recall only the barest outlines of it. The record of even the shortest most vivid dreams must therefore be made immediately on first awakening. The following is such a note of an early morning dream:

June, 1913.

A DREAM OF GEORGE BORROW

I dreamed that a great prize had been offered in the *Westminster Gazette* for an essay competition. The subject of the essay was to be *"The Books found in a Guest-chamber on a Week-end Visit."* I was on my way to a country house, and I wondered what books I should actually find in the bedroom that I should occupy in the house to which I

was going. . . . The big country house that I came
to was like O—— and I was taken upstairs on my
arrival to a room which I recognised as one in
which I had several times slept on visits there.
With my thoughts running on the essay I went
quickly to the bookshelf and looked eagerly at its
contents. There was a little row of books. Those
that I glanced at first were familiar to me, books
that I had read, novels I think, but I did not look
at them much, for they were of no use for my
special purpose, for the essay which was absorbing
my thoughts. I do not even remember what they
were; but I found towards the end of the shelf a
single volume entitled "Candide." Opening it, I
found a short preface which stated that this was a
quite newly discovered volume, hitherto unpub-
lished, and of remarkable interest; a continuation,
in fact, of "Candide's" story. I wondered if this
might not serve my turn and provide stuff for the
essay. I thought that it might, and began to turn
over its pages, when my eye fell on the last two
volumes standing in the little row. They were
dark-blue books, lettered in gold, and their title ran
"Mr. Petulengro, Vol. I, and Mr. Petulengro, Vol.
II." "Oh, wonderful and delightful discovery!"
I thought; "imagine finding two perfectly new
books by Borrow! A new 'Lavengro' and an un-
read and hitherto unheard-of 'Romany Rye'!
How unexpected and how enchanting! Could it be a
mistake?"—and I eagerly opened the two blue volumes. No, the promise held good. Here on the

first pages that I looked at were the familiar names, Jasper Petulengro, Mrs. Petulengro, Ursula. . . . Chapter headings, too, there were that seemed familiar, but that yet were all new!
The opening of my essay began to frame itself in my mind. The sentences with which it should begin, and in which I should tell of my discovery to the world, came quite readily, and I repeated them over to myself, though the importance of the fifty-guinea prize faded quite away in comparison with the excitement of the discovery that I had made. But then—alas! the dark-blue volumes themselves began to fade. I tried hard to keep them, but in vain; and I woke up to find that my favourite row of ''bedside books'' near at hand contained indeed the familiar slim green volumes which I knew so nearly by heart, but that ''Mr. Petulengro, Vol. I, and Mr. Petulengro, Vol. II,'' had disappeared with my dream.

I have been obliged to illustrate these studies of dreaming by notes of my own dreams. This has been unavoidable, because actual experience has been their foundation, and experience is my only qualification for writing on this subject. Where I could obtain records made by friends I have done so, but this has not been often, because few people will make these notes immediately on awaking from sleep, and records made after the lapse of some hours are of comparatively little value. An apology must, however, be made for using my own dreams in this way. We have all suffered at times from having to listen to the recital of dreams, which, though of scanty interest to the hearer, doubtless still possess for the teller some of the humour and the charm that they seemed to have in the night. Somewhat imperfectly remembered, and narrated in the cold light of day, these poor shadows of dreams convey none of their original glamour. No doubt from the earliest ages the same thing has happened; dreams have been dreamed, and have been re-told, and have wearied their hearers. Eighteen hundred years ago Epictetus laid down for his pupils the sound rule, which one amongst them evidently laid to heart and recorded: "Beware that thou never tell thy dreams, for notwithstanding thou mayst take pleasure in reciting the dreams of the night, the company will take little pleasure in hearing them." The moral, though a salutary one, now as it was then, is a discouraging maxim for a writer on dreams; but the reader, on the other hand, who is now duly forewarned, has a clear advantage over an unwilling listener, since it lies entirely within his own choice whether he reads, or whether he skips, the written dream.

CHAPTER V

Memory begets Judgment and Fancy: Judgment begets the strength and structure, and Fancy begets the ornaments of a Poem.—HOBBES, *Leviathan*.

Some of the difficulties that we meet with in remembering our dreams have been described, and the part that memory plays in the process of recalling and recording them. The materials out of which dreams are built up, and the part taken in their building by memory, imagination, and by other mental faculties, must now be considered.

The basis of all our dreams is furnished by memory from things that have been seen, heard and remembered. In the dream state, memory is characterised by greatly increased vigour and often a scene casually glanced at in the course of a journey, and half or quite forgotten as we hurry by in railway or motor, will reproduce itself in our dreams with a wealth of remembered detail and with a precision that was absent from the original fugitive impression, and may remain imprinted on the dream memory for years, a picture unfaded by time. A thousand such impressions, which at the moment hardly seem to make any mark on our

minds, reappear in this way with extreme distinctness. "It is a strange but undoubted fact that
the memory can be charged with lasting impressions of things seen which pass through the visual
sense unnoticed and unknown of it."[1]

If memory acts as the builder, the provider of
the material from which dreams are made, imagination may be looked upon as their architect. Imagination transforms all these remembered facts and
impressions, and combines them afresh, using them
to create for us totally new surroundings, but it
does not, and cannot, act without that basis of experience that is supplied by memory. It makes
free use of all that we have gleaned from travel,
from books, from things heard; but we do not—at
least I certainly do not in my dreams—conceive of
a world that is outwardly very unlike our own, or
of beings of a new and wholly different order from
ourselves. Even the gifts and accomplishments
which we acquire only in our dreams, and which
may not be ours by day, are possessed by other
men and women. Gifts of music, of beautiful motion, of oratory, may be ours only in sleep, and like
supermen we may master the hardest of these
things with effortless ease, but they are all gifts
that belong to men like ourselves, things which men
of our own race have done and can do. Our powers of flying, and of overcoming distances of time
and space in our dreams, are the exceptions to this
rule. These are powers which belong to no mortal

[1] F. Greenwood, "Imagination in Dreams."

by day, and it is perhaps for that very reason that we hold these dreams so dear. As a general rule we do not in our dreams even invent new trees or new flowers, and although the combinations made by imagination result sometimes in dream scenes that have all the charm of originality and of a certain strange foreignness, still our dream world is on the whole a world resembling in most of its outward characteristics the world we live in, and in the greater number of our dreams even the details of that familiar world are faithfully reproduced.

No change that takes place in any of the mental faculties during sleep is more remarkable or more certainly attested than the heightening of the faculty of imagination. The great increase of imaginative force that is conferred upon us is what gives our dreams their greatest charm, the vividness of our dream images being in many cases far greater than that of the mental images that we can form by day. I believe that the dream mind has in itself a much more intense power of imaginative vision than our normal mind possesses. It is, moreover, free, as many writers on dreams have noted, to work out its effects without the interference of contrary or irrelevant ideas that hamper the imaginative force of the waking mind. By day the imagination is often distracted by other thoughts, and cannot fully concentrate itself upon a single image; it works in a stricter subjection to the reasoning faculty, and in obedience also to the laws that govern our universe and, only when the memory of these is partly lifted off in sleep, the imagination is free to create new conditions which do not depend upon these laws. Difficulties, which must seem insuperable to the normal mind, which is obliged to think of things as happening in time, and to regard everything under the conditions of time and space that are familiar to us, are no longer insurmountable in dreams. Men have built up "laws which seem to correspond with the phenomena of succession and slow sequence which are part of our observations of nature." [1] In our dreams we pass directly into a condition where our ordinary conceptions of the sequence of time and relative distance are done away with, where these laws no longer exist for us, and where entirely different conditions prevail. Distance is annihilated in our dreams, which take no account of the continents that may intervene between us and the remote spot to which our thoughts may fly, and to which we may be instantly transported as on the Princess Badoura's magic carpet. In this respect, at least, the world of dreams differs fundamentally from the world we know by day.

The thought of a certain lake in Kashmir flashes into my dream mind, and instantly I find myself there, lying as I often do, in the reed-thatched house-boat in which I live and voyage on the lake. A fractional part of the journey thither may or may not come into the dream, but the preliminary of travelling is, as often as not, altogether omitted.

[1] Bishop Westcott.

One has only to think of a place, and one is there. Sir Philip Sidney was perhaps thinking of such dreams as these when he wrote of imagination as the faculty "that flies from one Indies to the other." Just as completely as our conceptions of distances disappear in dreams, so are our conceptions of time swept away. The thought of some historic event may carry us back in a dream across the centuries, and make us live for a little while in another age, the dream imagination accomplishing for us in an instant the task that the historian achieves in many pages. Like the clairvoyant described by M. Maeterlinck, we "do not feel what the future is, or distinguish it from other senses."[1]

De Quincey describes how in such dreams he saw ". . . a crowd of ladies, a festival and dances. And I heard it said, or I said it to myself, 'These are English ladies from the unhappy times of Charles I. These are the wives and daughters of those who met in peace, and sat at the same tables, and were allied by marriage or by blood; and yet after a certain day in August, 1642, never smiled upon each other again, nor met but in the field of battle; and at Marston Moor, at Newbury, or at Naseby, cut asunder all ties of blood by the cruel sabre, and washed away in blood the memory of ancient friendship.' The ladies danced, and looked as lovely as the court of George IV. Yet I knew, even in my dream, that they had been in the grave

[1] Maeterlinck, "The Unknown Guest."

for nearly two centuries. This pageant would suddenly dissolve; and at a clapping of hands, would be heard the heart-quaking sound of *Consul Romanum:* and immediately came sweeping by in gorgeons paludaments, Paulus or Marius, girt round by a company of centurions, with the crimson tunic hoisted on a spear, and followed by the *alalagmos* of the Roman legions.''

In dreams such transitions from time present backwards to time long past, and onwards to time yet to come, are lightly made; they present no difficulties to the imagination that is not bound by the laws that govern our thoughts of time by day. The following is taken from a short note of such a transition dream, dated January, 1915:

In my dream I am looking across the grasslands and cornfields of a countryside that seems half, but only half, familiar to me. By degrees I realise that I am looking at the actual fields of Waterloo. As I gaze at them I see a thin line of men hurrying over the crest of the low, grey hill in front of me. They are coming over at a running pace, and I can see the ancient red uniforms of the British soldiers. Waterloo is being fought and I am there watching it! And a guide standing by my side, like the chorus in a Greek play, is telling me what the distant scenes of the battle mean. From very, very far away the faint sound of cheering comes across the plain; the guide tells me to listen and to hear whether the sound has ''the long-drawn-out note of the British hurrah,'' or if it is the sharp punctuated note of the Hochs, that would signify the coming of Blucher's army.

A few seconds later the scene of the dream and its century had changed, and it was carried forward into a future which, at the moment when this note was written, seemed infinitely far off; for it now took place in the public square of a strange foreign city, where under innumerable flags, and with triumphant music, and a procession of the soldiers of all nations, the Peace which was at last to end the Great War was being celebrated.

The annihilation by the imagination of the sense of time, separating us from the past and from the future, is a mental operation very similar to that which imagination accomplishes for us when we try to reconstruct an event in history. There are pages in which great historians have lighted up historic scenes, giving them the force of living reality; but, left to ourselves, how few of us can impart life to history in this way? Memory supplies the materials for both the mental picture that we try to form and for the dream picture, but I think that the impression made upon the mind by the dream is often far more vivid than the other. No written records, however, of such dreams give any idea of the extraordinary sense of reality that they impart at the moment; and unfortunately many of us who see vividly in our dreams are unable to record our dreams at all, or are but little able to convey any adequate impression of their force by means of written words.

Amongst dreams which have been clearly suggested by a definite act of memory are the numerous dreams which have their origin in words or phrases that have been preserved by memory in the hinterland of our thoughts, and which start into prominence as soon as we are asleep.

Memory has only to bring up from these stores, and to suggest to the dream imagination, some remembered word, some place-name or some familiar phrase, and the idea thus suggested is at once seized upon, and the imagination begins its constructive work. A sentence, for instance, which is familiar to us, is often the opening from which a whole dream story will grow. The following is the briefest example that I can find in my notes of a dream that grew in this way out of a remembered phrase:

November, 1916.

I was standing in the midst of a great crowd in the open space of the Mall in front of Buckingham Palace. Like the rest of the world, I had come out to see the remnant of the army of Belgium who had survived the Great War, and who, peace having been declared, had been brought to London to receive the welcome of our King and people. The crowd about me was so dense that for a time I could only see the shoulders of the people near me, but presently it parted a little, and I could see an army of short dark men, dressed in splendid uniforms with touches of scarlet about them, whilst others were in uniforms almost covered with gold.

Some one standing just behind me (as the "guide" so often stands) said, "Why, they are all *chamarré d'or,* like the Guards' band at a State dinner or ball in the Palace," but I was so sorely disappointed that I turned away almost in tears. "Oh, but I did not come to see *this,*" I said; "these men look merely like dressed-up dolls!" and indeed they were not in the least like the war-worn soldiers whom I had pictured, and who had fought and suffered so long. In the sharpness of my disappointment I awoke. I began as usual writing down the dreams of the night. Something about this particular dream haunted me, something that was certainly missing from it that would explain it, and I lay awake wondering—whilst some other part of my mind was meanwhile at work, actively searching for the missing connection or idea—for a refrain which I felt somehow echoed through the dream itself, but which I could not recall. And then suddenly it flashed back to me in the words: "But what went ye out for to see? A man clothed in soft raiment? Behold, they that are clothed in soft raiment dwell in kings' houses. But what went ye out for to see?" Kings' houses—those were the familiar words round which the dream had crystallised, and the origin of it at once became clear. The crowd outside the King's palace! What had we come out to see? The dream imagination did the rest, and made up the brief dream story.

Just in the same way a place-name often makes the starting-point from which a dream of travel originates.

I had asked in a furniture shop one day the name of a folding tea-table, and had been told that it was a "Sutherland table." "Why Sutherland?" I had idly wondered at the moment. In my sleep the memory of the word recurred, but it was no longer associated with the idea of the table, but with the map of Northern Scotland, and the place of Sutherland in it, and, as so often happens in a dream, no sooner had I thought of the name than I found myself travelling thither.

I was in a large railway carriage arranged not at all on the plan of our own carriages, but more as I imagine an American car to be arranged. I noted the curious sleeping-berths that looked foreign and unfamiliar to me. It seemed that the journey was taking us to the extreme north of Scotland. An Italian woman of the poorer class was travelling with a party of friends, some of them foreigners, one of whom talked to me in English. He explained to me that their personal luggage and all their household furniture had been sent on by a cheaper conveyance. I saw from their shapes that the bundles that the Italian woman had with her, both on and under the seat, were evidently the cooking utensils from which probably she could not bear to be parted; these were tied up in large handkerchiefs. She had no change of clothes or any travelling comforts with her, and the thought crossed my mind that I too must be rather travel-stained, for the journey had already lasted some days and nights. Being tired, my thoughts flew longingly on to my destination . . . and lo! I had arrived there! . . . I found myself sitting on the lawn outside a large house at a tea-table round which my hosts and their numerous guests were gathered and were talking together. My hostess was describing graphically a long motor-tour that they had lately made, which had taken them to a place in the neighbouring county of Sutherland, to a wonderful castle, in which the owner had collected together a number of priceless Italian pictures, and a library of books that would make the fortune of any European collector. How these extraordinary treasures had been obtained was a mystery which my host and hostess did nothing to solve. My host whispered the word "loot," but evidently did not wish to divulge any more than he could help about either the owner of the collection or the place where it was kept. The names of both person and place were hurriedly mentioned, but in an aside—and so murmured that I could not catch them. I asked for them to be repeated, but again they were so slurred over that I had no better success. I tried various devices to get them repeated afresh more clearly, but in vain. The owner's name, as I caught it imperfectly, sounded like Mor. I asked for an atlas, thinking that a study of the county of Sutherland might enable me to find out approximately the whereabouts of the strange castle and mysterious collection, for I now felt determined that whatever happened I would go there and investigate these treasures for myself. But whenever I introduced the subject I was quietly put off by my hosts, and whilst I was still making plans an interruption occurred. Alas! I never found the way to the wonderful castle, although the dream of which this was the opening was a very long one.

.　.　.　.　.　.　.　.　.　.

A fresh impression too easily distracts our attention in a dream, and imagination beguiles us from the track we were following, and leads us down each new path that opens before us.

Although I find that in my own dreams a consecutive story is often pursued fairly steadily to its end, the experience of many people whom I have asked about dreams is that the centre of interest is continually shifting, and that a dream story is therefore very seldom complete or consistent. The power of continued close attention appears in many cases to be missing; and in this respect, at any rate, the imagination seems to work in sleep without the check that keeps it steadily directed on to one line of thought by day.

It is often assumed that in sleep all the mental faculties except imagination are dormant; and that the heightened powers that imagination acquires in dreams is due to the suspension of the other faculties that control it by day. I have tried to show that will-power does not come to a standstill, and that memory acts with increased force, and it should not be difficult to prove that in most dreams. if not in all, the reasoning faculty also operates with varying degrees of power. Indeed, unless we assume such co-operation, the construction and sequence of many dreams could not possibly be accounted for. The making of a coherent story in a dream requires the participation of the same functions of mind as those that enable us to construct such a story by day. The great diversity of dreams is seen in the fact that, whilst some show in a very high degree the powers of reasoning and constructive ability, others would clearly take a very low place in such a scale; but I believe that in all our dreams we make some attempt to reason. Even in the very incoherent dreams, which are the dreams of more or less disordered sleep, in which the restraint that is generally imposed by the reason upon the imagination seems at first sight to have been lifted off, if we consider the matter attentively we see that reason is not really wholly in abeyance. Our reasoning in such disordered dreams may be very illogical, very perverse, but the reason is nevertheless at work trying hard to synthesise the scattered incoherent expressions that come floating up to the surface of the mind when we sleep. Exactly where the province of reason ends, and that of imagination begins, I do not know: the question must be left to philosophers to settle, for students of dreams are certainly not agreed about it. Whilst one writer looks on dreams as being simply the outcome of man's "strenuous instinct to rea-

son,'' another sees them as the creation of imagination freed to a great extent from the control of the
reasoning faculty. The truth probably is that we
judge in this matter, as in so many others, largely
according to the nature of our own experience, and
see but one side of a shield which has its golden as
well as its silver side. A man whose dream life
is very full and imaginative realises chiefly that
side of dreaming; dreams are to such men what
they were to Keats, a ''great key to golden palaces

ay, to all the mazy world of silvery enchantment.'' On the other hand, a man of scientific
training and habit of thought, whose dream life has
perhaps little in common with the visions of the
poet, and who has learned to look upon all forms
of mental activity as reducible at last to reasoning,
will naturally attribute his dreams to the operation
of that faculty. But both aspects may surely be true.
In dreams, as in waking life, imagination is continually forming in our minds new images which
have not been previously experienced, or experienced only partially or in different combinations;
and reason is equally busy all the time synthesis-
ing into unity these images and concepts of the
mind. We do not always recognise it as reason in
our dreams, because its results are so illogical, the
reasoning that it achieves is so bad, and we are accustomed to judge of reason by its capacity to draw
logical inferences. But that is where waking reason and dream reason differ widely from each
other; for many of the facts and memories that

help us to arrive at logical conclusions by day are absent from our dream consciousness, and thus reason, working upon insufficient materials, comes to conclusions that are false and absurd.

Reasoning that is logical, as far as the facts in the possession of the dream mind allow it to be so, is a feature of most dreams, and indeed it seems as if, in the production of every dream, reason must take some share. Besides the general offices that it performs in all our dreams, levelling difficulties and explaining away inconsistencies that arise, it appears to be responsible for the curious debates that so often take place in them when some one in the dream advances arguments which we try to meet. We are, I conclude, really furnishing both argument and reply. My notes of dreams are full of such conversations, and often, like Dr. Johnson, in the dream that he described, I have the worst of the argument and have to fall back on admiring the readiness of my dream opponent. Sometimes, but more rarely, I appear to be wiser or more convincing than he is. The logical faculty is not very strongly developed in me, but it does not seem to have quite deserted me in the following odd little dream:

I was sitting by the side of a young man who was explaining to me his serious financial troubles. I did not know him; he was a red-haired, plain but pleasant youth, and was clearly very much worried. He had before him a paper on which there were written columns of figures, at which I looked over his shoulder. These were, it appeared, the sums, at varying rates per cent., that he had arranged to pay to money lenders.

"Can you possibly explain to me how much I've got to pay, and how much I've got left?" asked the youth.

"I don't understand a bit," I said, "but as far as I can make out from this paper you seem to have covenanted to pay a hundred per cent. per annum."

"Yes," he said, "that's about it, I expect. Doesn't it seem to you right and fair?"

I felt dreadfully puzzled (as I always am by figures).

"I don't know," I said, "but I think that seems all right for once, doesn't it?—a hundred per cent. once, but not a hundred per cent. per annum——"

"Oh," said the young man, "by ——! Is that how it strikes you?"

In dreams of argument such as these, different faculties of the mind seem to be at work behind the scenes, prompting and moving in a life-like manner the puppets that occupy the dream stage.

Confronted by our own wisdom in this way, which makes it seem not our own but another's, we may, when we awake, have the agreeable sense that the best of the argument, the brightest of the replies, have really been ours; a great advantage possessed by the dream over real life, in which the consciousness that ours has only been at best *l'esprit de l'escalier,* so often effectually keeps in check any tendency to undue satisfaction with ourselves.

CHAPTER VI

THE "SUPER-DREAM"

There are some who claim to have lived longer and more richly than their neighbours; when they lay asleep they claim they were still active; and among the treasures of memory that all men review for their amusement, these count in no second place the harvests of their dreams.—R. L. STEVENSON, *A Chapter on Dreams.*

A more curious and much rarer type of dream than any of those that have hitherto been described, but which is attested by perfectly reliable witnesses, is what may be called the super-dream; in which the dream mind, working beyond its ordinary level of capacity, has actually solved problems that have defeated the efforts of the normal mind in its waking hours. The instance of Condorcet, who in such a dream solved a mathematical problem, the answer to which he had vainly sought by day, has been often quoted; and Condorcet's experience was almost exactly repeated in the case of my father Nevil Story-Maskelyne. The mathematical problem that had baffled him came into the treatise on crystallography on which he was engaged. After working at it for many hours he was obliged to leave it unsolved and to go to bed. He fell into a deep sleep, and in the course of a long dream the answer to the problem came to him.

He often described this to me and told me how in an early hour of the morning he awoke and wrote down the solution that the dream had given him, and anxiously tested its correctness.

A friend writes of her very similar experience in solving mathematical difficulties in her sleep "On more than one occasion when studying for examinations I worked for two or three days at a problem without arriving at the solution, and finally worked it in my dreams with such clearness that I was able to write down the correct result quite easily on awaking. On occasions during my schooldays the same thing used to happen, and if I met with very hard sums and riders I used to put pencil and paper by my bedside so as to be ready to write down the answer if it came to me in my sleep." Henri Fabre, in his "Souvenirs Entomologiques," explains that sleep in his case was often a state which did not suspend the mind's activity but actually quickened it, and in sleep he was able at times to solve mathematical problems with which he had struggled by day. "A brilliant beacon flares up in my brain, and then I jump from my bed, light my lamp and write down the solution the memory of which would otherwise be lost; like flashes of lightning these gleams vanish as suddenly as they appear."

These cases, though uncommon, are not isolated ones; other equally reliable witnesses have told of their similar experiences; and though these seem specially striking when the problems grappled with by the dream mind are the problems of such an exact science as mathematics, there is nothing in their occurrence that is out of harmony with what we know, or with what the latest researches of science teach us, about the mental faculties in the dream state. Reason is, we believe, continually at work in dreams, and we know that in this state imagination works with greatly increased powers. Imagination is an essential element in the attainment of any great intellectual result; and progress in mathematical knowledge, as in all scientific research, has been largely due to "provisional explanations constructed by the imagination, such explanations being framed in accordance with known facts." One great difference between these "super-dreams" and the ordinary dream is that a sufficiently clear remembrance of essential facts is carried over into the dream state to enable the dream reason to draw correct inferences, whereas in most dreams it has to work on more or less insufficient data and consequently often comes to wrong conclusions. Armed with the necessary facts, reason in the super-dream works correctly and powerfully, and at the same time imagination supplies the other essential element that the thinker needs. Thought alone is not sufficient for most operations of the mind; imagination is also required. In every case of the kind that I have met with, the solution that has thus been arrived at in the dream seems to the dreamer not to be the product of his own reasoning powers, but to be a conclusion arrived at independently of himself, like a light flashed on to his mind from without, illuminating the difficulty that had seemed hopeless to his normal mind by day. This type of dream, with its strange faculty of insight or intuition, has been realised perhaps more often by men of letters than by men of science, although it must be in any case a rare experience. The dream in which Coleridge composed ''Kubla Khan'' may possibly be looked upon with some doubt, because in his case sleep was at times induced and influenced by opium, but there seems no reason to question the fact that the conception of the poem came to him in a dream, and that a part of it, at any rate, was written down from memory directly afterwards. Various instances of creative dreams have been related. A striking example of an original and very dramatic story which was entirely the creation of a dream was told me lately by a writer who has attained a distinguished place among modern novelists. At the time when the dream occurred he was engaged on a book which was absorbing all his time and thoughts; about two-thirds of this had already been written, and it was making steady progress to completion, when one night he experienced a dream of extraordinary force and vividness. In this dream a story of a most dramatic nature was partially unfolded, and on following nights it was continued and completed. He dreamed and re-dreamed the story. The whole plot, the scenes of the drama and its characters, were so clearly realised, and made upon the dreamer so insistent an impression, that he could not free himself from the memory of them; they came between him and his other work, and he was at last obliged to lay this on one side until he had fully written down the dream story. He is, he explained, a rather slow worker, attaining the effects that he seeks by dint of patient care, but when he began to write down the dream it seemed to be like a tale that was told to him rather than a thing of his own creation. The story as he wrote it certainly conveys the impression, not of invented scenes and happenings, but rather of things that had actually been witnessed by the narrator. This may, however, of course, be due, not to the curious manner in which it had its origin, but to the graphic power of the novelist. Very similar to his experience were the dream creations which were so fully described by Robert Louis Stevenson in his essay called "A Chapter on Dreams." [1] In this essay, which gives a most lucid account of his whole dream life, he described the process of inventive dreaming from which many of his stories originated. So completely did these dreams seem to him to be an inspiration from outside himself, the operation of faculties apart from the workings of his normal mind and working at a higher level, that he speaks of them as being the handiwork of the "Little People," Brownies of the mind, who—whilst he slept—bestirred themselves to construct and elaborate for him the plots of his stories, far better tales, he declared, than any that he could invent for

[1] R. L. Stevenson, "Across the Plains."

himself by day. He gives in this essay the outlines of one such story, of which he says truly that
it would be hard to better the dramatic effective-
ness of its situations. The plot of the dream story
hinged upon the hidden motive of the woman who
played the leading part in the little drama; and until its very end that secret was kept.

"The dreamer . . . had no guess whatever at
this motive—the hinge of the whole well-invented
plot—until the instant of its highly dramatic decla-
ration. It was not his tale; it was the Little
People's! And observe; not only was the secret
kept, the story was told with really guileful craftsmanship. . . . I am awake now, and I know this
trade; and yet I cannot better it . . . the more I
think of it, the more I am moved to press upon the
world my question, who are the Little People?
They are near connections of the dreamer's, beyond doubt.   They share plainly in his training: they have plainly learned like him to build the
scheme of a consistent story and to arrange emotion in progressive order; only I think they have
more talent; and one thing is beyond doubt, they
can tell him a story piece by piece, like a serial,
and keep him all the while in ignorance of where
they aim."

What indeed are these "dream-builders"? If
we could but answer this question satisfactorily,
we should solve the most baffling problems of our
dreams. This power of the dream mind not only
to construct a dramatic story, but to conceal from

us till the very end the *dénouement* to which the story led up, what a mystery it reveals! How does this thing happen? We know that it does happen, for, though our own dreams are far from being such remarkable ones as those described by Stevenson, and though they lack all the craftsmanship and finish of his, yet we too have experienced the same thrill of wonder when a secret carefully hidden from us till the end has suddenly been disclosed.

The suggestion made in the earlier part of this chapter as to the main difference between the ordinary dreams and super-dreams does not here suffice. It is inadequate to account for mental processes such as these. For here, far more even than in our dreams of argument, a dual consciousness or personality seems to be present; here again the curious sense is felt that some one not quite oneself, some one with rather different faculties from one's own, but yet an integral part of self, is at work, taking a hand in the business. Facts that we do not know are in his possession, and the answer to the riddle of the dream story is within the knowledge of this other self though it is hidden from ourselves. Stevenson realised that this other self was intimately related to the dreamer, trained as he himself was trained, but able, he believed, to do something which he himself could not do, or to do it better; and to this same mysterious other self I imagine that the mathematician also owes the dream solution of his problem.

These and many equally curious and interesting

experiences which are nowadays occupying the attention of men of science seem to require the assumption of a secondary consciousness existing side by side with our ordinary personal consciousness, and indeed, unless we can assume the presence of such a divided personality or consciousness, it seems almost impossible to conceive how certain processes of the mind are carried out in the dream state or in the hypnotic state.

The consideration of this most difficult aspect of the subject belongs to a later chapter, and, although it can only be dealt with imperfectly by an observer who has not the necessary knowledge of psychology, it would be impossible to deal at all thoroughly with the question of dreams, unless this aspect is considered.

Before passing on to other questions, it is curious to note the attitude that many people, writers and others, adopt with regard to dream experiences, which, like those described above, are outside the common range of experience, and which do not chance to have come under their own immediate observation. Dreamers who have actually had these uncommon experiences know from first-hand knowledge that, strange as they may seem, such dreams occur and must be taken into account when problems concerning the activity of the mind in sleep, or the possibility of a divided consciousness or dual personality in man, are considered. But whereas a man's careful and straightforward statement about the processes of his waking thoughts would be accepted without questioning, it is more than likely that if he should make an equally careful statement about his dreams he will find that this is looked upon very doubtfully by his fellows. Even a philosopher like M. Bergson, having stated the theory that in general "dreams create nothing," finds it necessary to explain away the case of such creative dreams as Stevenson's by saying that the dreamer was probably in a psychical state in which it would have been difficult to say whether he were asleep or awake, for "when the mind creates, when it is capable of making the effort to organise and synthesise which is necessary in order to triumph over a difficulty, to solve a problem, or to produce a work of imagination, we are not really asleep."[1] This summary way of dealing with facts or records which clash awkwardly with theories is noted here only because this attitude is rather often found in books about dreaming, but it is a curious attitude to adopt towards Stevenson's very deliberate and very careful analysis of his dream life over a period of years. If in pursuing another study we found that carefully recorded facts did not conform to a theory that we had formed, we should probably concede that the theory might be either incorrect or not sufficiently elastic.

"The question whether anything can be known is to be settled not by arguing but by trying,"[2] and the inductive method of arriving at truth by means

[1] Henri Bergson, "Revue Scientifique," Paris, June, 1901.
[2] Bacon, "Novum Organon."

of experiment rather than by logic advocated by the
great philosopher is still the method that it is safest
to follow if our conclusions are to be sound. It is,
of course, the absence of sufficient accurately recorded facts concerning dreams that has made it
natural that philosophers should build up their
theories concerning them without an adequately
wide foundation. And so once again we are
brought round to the need for a clearing house of
dreams, whose widely gathered stores of observation would be available to correct or to confirm the
theories about the working of the dream mind that
science may hereafter form.

CHAPTER VII

SYMBOLISM IN DREAMS AND THE SIGNIFICANCE OF DREAMS IN TRADITION

Our advanced ideas are really in great part but the latest fashion in "definition"—a more accurate expression, by words in *logy* and *ism*, of sensations which men and women have vaguely grasped for centuries.—THOMAS HARDY, *Tess of the Tubervilles.*

The theory of the symbolic nature of dreams underlies the teaching of all modern psychology. The discovery of this curious characteristic of the dream mind was first made by Freud, and on it he laid great emphasis. In the course of his discoveries in the unconscious he was the first to formulate the theory that beneath the dream itself a subconscious process has been at work fashioning the conscious dream; and he insists further that every dream, if fully analysed, would be found to have a symbolic nature and to be always the allegorical representation of the fulfilment of a sex wish.

I believe that there are indeed many dreams which are symbolic representations of some underlying mental experience, some wish, or trouble, or some pleasanter thought which has occupied our mind by day, and which is transmitted by the dream mind. We can, if we analyse our dreams, trace in certain of them a symbolism under the figure of which such thoughts and moods seem to be represented; but my experience convinces me that it is not true to say that all dreams are symbolic, any more than we can accept as of universal truth the Freudian theory that they are all symbols of repressed desire.

When I examine my own dreams I find that in the cases where these seem to be symbolic the symbolism appears generally to be of a simple and direct nature, relating the dream to some mood that I have experienced, or some problem that I have met with, and it is often fairly easy to trace this idea, which the dream represents in an allegorical form. In this modified sense it seems evident that many dreams are symbolical.

The true Freudian psycho-analyst would not, however, be content with such an analysis as this; for he insists that every dream, if completely analysed, would be revealed as the symbolic fulfilment of a "wish" which is always a "sex wish." He would not accept the definition that "a dream may be the symbolical expression of almost any thought"[1]—a definition which perfectly sums up the conclusions to which my own limited experience has led me.

In the case of dreams whose form suggests that they may have a symbolic character, it is interesting to try to trace, with the help of our knowledge of our own mental experience, the underlying idea that the dream probably symbolises; and this idea, and the memories that help to make up the "mani-

[1] Morton Prince, "The Unconscious," p. 221.

fest content'' of the dream, can in many cases be
easily recognised. We are, however, under an obvious disadvantage if we try further to apply the
Freudian theories of analysis to our dreams, and
to investigate their "latent content"; for we are
warned at the outset that it is difficult, if not practically impossible, to trace this for ourselves, and
to discern the repressed thoughts from which they
spring; because the normal mind, whose office it is
to suppress such thoughts from our consciousness,
acts always as "censor," and forbids our becoming aware of them and prevents our recognising
the secret impulses which dreams symbolise.

"The work of the censor is so complete that the
immoral, that is to say unsocial, nature of the
wishes constantly striving for utterance is absolutely hidden by him from the dreamer's conscious
life, and can be revealed only by psycho-analytic research." [1]

Only, it would seem, by way of the new confes-
sional can we hope to arrive at the innermost truth
about ourselves, and the process appears in some
cases to be a somewhat tedious one, and possibly
of doubtful usefulness.[2]

[1] Lay, "Man's Unconscious Conflict."

[2] The process of psycho-analysis varies in length "according to
circumstances from one sitting to hundreds. Daily talks for eight
months or a year may be necessary to resolve some of the problems
brought by people who are physically sound, according to medical
examination, while a single sitting has been known to remove a
serious difficulty that has endured for years."—Lay, "Man's Unconscious Conflict," p. 149.

A mere student cannot weigh and judge all the evidence bearing on the "censor" theory, but a plea for the exercise of sober judgment and common sense in our study of this subject and the conclusions that we form, does not seem to be unneeded.

It has been said that symbolism of a simple kind is evidently to be found in some dreams, representing in a changed form a thought which has occupied our mind by day. In the following dream record the symbolism seems to be of a very direct nature:

A little party of people were gathered together in a large room. It was night-time, lamps were lighted, and some of the older ones were playing "patience." I was sitting near the fire with a book reading, and looking out through the long windows which opened on to a wide lawn flooded with moonlight beyond which the arches of a cloister could be seen. A number of girls and boys were dancing on the lawn; as I watched the dancing figures I slipped away from "myself" and ran out to join them; I glanced back from the open window for a moment at the group under the lamplight, at the patience players, and at myself sitting sedately in my low chair with my book open on my knee.

We danced hand in hand in a long chain running very lightly and fast, passing in and out of the shadows of the arches, and out into the moonlit spaces again. The lightness and slenderness of my body delighted me, and as I looked down at my feet I said, laughing, "The old ones by the fire would think that these silk shoes were much too thin for dancing at night upon the grass.''

A youth danced by my side, but he was without importance in the dream and did not interest me; ''only,'' I thought, ''I should not be at all in the movement if I were partnerless.'' A girl in the chain of dancers began to tell a story, another took up the recital, and so the dream went on.

As a student of the works of Freud and his followers I fully realise the nature of the various interpretations—most of them unpleasant—which may be read into this dream, the repressed thoughts and complexes to which it may be attributed. The explanation of it that I believe to be a true and sufficient one is of a simpler nature. To me the dream relates to a mood which is familiar to all of us as the years pass and as age comes nearer to us, a mood when we gaze tenderly, but a little wistfully, at the grace and youth of a new generation. I am very content; I sit happily with my books, and I watch with delight the young flying figures that are playing tennis on the lawn, or dancing, but the pleasure is accompanied sometimes with a little sigh of remembrance, for it was very good once upon a time to be young, and in my dream I am young again.

The dream that is recorded on page 163, Chapter XIII, is used there as an illustration of the working of the two factors of our dual consciousness in a dream, and has its place in the argument of that

chapter. It may be referred to here from another
point of view. In this dream certain household
possessions, some silk curtains and pieces of brocade had been found out of doors upon the ground,
soiled by rain and melting snow. I was distressed
by their condition and absorbed in the care of getting them dried and cleaned. I took part in the
dream in a dual capacity—(1) as the "dreamer"
who found the things in the snow and was busied
in restoring them, and (2) as an outsider, a critic,
who argued with the dreamer, questioning the reality of the worry that was so oppressive, and insist-
ing that the trouble was only "dream trouble."

It was suggested to me by one who has brought
his great knowledge of psychology to the science of
healing, to whom I had been allowed to send some
of my dream notes, that I had not dwelt upon the
symbolisms in dreams, or laid sufficient stress on
this aspect of them. He wrote· "Your dream of
the brocade and silk curtains strongly suggests to
me a symbolism and reference to some mental experience (repressed thoughts, etc.) of your inner
life. I would not pretend to guess what these were,
but will leave you to your own psycho-analysis,
which might show what 'soiled' thoughts you may
have had. I feel quite sure that symbolisms do
occur, for I have observed in mv subjects such obvious ones that they needed no psycho-analysis.
However, to hold that all dreams are symbolic, as
Freud does, is to me absurd."

My own analysis of the dream suggests to me a

different symbolism which, although a simple one, accounts, I think, for the mental disturbance that the dream represented.

Some time previously the old country house in which I live had come to me by inheritance. I have always looked on myself as caretaker or guardian of it and of its contents. Difficulties arising from war-time conditions in giving adequate care to these, and the need for special precautions as to insurance, etc., were often in my mind. I am convinced that these anxieties were symbolised in the dreams, and that they are the explanation of the "dream trouble" which obsessed me.

. . . . . .

Belief in a symbolic and prophetic significance attaching to dreams is revealed in some form or other in the religions and early literature of all races. Dreams filled a great place in the beliefs and traditions of primitive peoples: the strangeness of the dream life, so like and yet so unlike the normal life of man, seems to have haunted his thoughts from the beginning of time. The Hebrew people were in no way singular in looking on dreams as allegorical in character and as the channel through which divinely inspired messages and warnings were conveyed to men, and in setting a high value on the gifts of those who seemed able to interpret their hidden meanings. Underlying these beliefs there was always the conviction that in sleep or in the transition time between sleeping and waking the mind is especially sensitive to influences external to itself, and lends itself readily as a medium of communication with the unseen.

From the dawn of history down to the present day these beliefs have appeared and reappeared, and would seem to be deeply rooted in the minds of men, since they have survived all changes in men's faiths. In a primitive form they linger on to this day. Fragments of the old soothsayer's lore are still to be found in our villages, and the wise woman can tell you, if she will, what your dream of last night portends. In these interpretations the event foreshadowed is generally in sharp contrast to the thing dreamed of. "Dream of joy, and wake to sorrow," and "Dream of frost, and dread fire," are samples of a dream lore that has the weight of long tradition in our countryside. It cannot be only amongst primitive countryfolk that interest and belief in the significance of dreams are still to be found, for a book purporting to give the meanings of two thousand four hundred dreams lies before me. If its contents prove disappointing to the seeker after enlightenment, in quantity at least it leaves nothing to be desired; few of us, however active our dream life may be, could ask for more. The old conceptions about dreams and their prophetic significance are probably to be found nowadays only among the uneducated; but for centuries the same beliefs were part of the general creed, accepted alike by the simple and the learned; and it was only in later times, when scientific knowledge had advanced and reasoning had become more critical, that the old unquestioning acceptance of such traditions gave way, and there sprang up among educated men a profound distrust of everything that savoured of superstitions from which they had but lately freed themselves. Their distrust was indeed so great that the dread of superstition became at times as unreasoning as the older dread of heresy. And so it came about that, because dreams had formerly been looked upon as a recognised part of the supernatural machinery of the world, any discussion of the phenomena of dreaming was vetoed and their study condemned, lest superstition should again lift up its head or have any say with regard to them. But generations come and go, and with each generation the point of view alters. Now once more philosophers are occupied with the problem of the significance of dreams. The study of dreams is their especial province, and, whilst we pay all due honour to their difficult researches in the field of the unconscious, it is not too much to say that some of their subtle dream interpretations seem to ask for as great a measure of faith on the part of the unlearned as was ever demanded by the interpreters of old.

CHAPTER VIII

DREAM PLACES

My dreams . are of architecture and of buildings—cities abroad, which I have never seen, and hardly hope to see. I have traversed, for the seeming length of a natural day, Rome, Amsterdam, Paris, Lisbon—their churches, palaces, market places, shops, suburbs, ruins, with an inexpressible sense of delight— a map-like distinctness of trace—and a daylight vividness of vision that was all but being awake.—CHARLES LAMB.

There are a few dreamers who are privileged to revisit often a dream country that becomes as familiar to them as any country that they know by day. In a little book called "Dreams in War-Time," Mr. E. M. Martin has described in detail a countryside to which his dreams give him access. It is, he says, "a country I know well, and that is as real to me, and as dear to me, as any of the fields and woods I knew and loved when a child. In it there are dream woods, where I can lose my way as contentedly as in the New Forest, for dream squirrels, ponies, deer, and dogs follow me in friendly fashion along untrodden paths; dream houses where I am by turns host, by turns guest; dream castles (sometimes in ruins, but more often in all their old state and splendour), where every room is familiar to me; dream rivers, along whose sleepy tide I have floated through lazy summer days; dream villages, in whose inn parlour I am a welcome guest."

102

Few of us are quite as fortunate as Mr. Martin has been in the matter of dreams, for until the war intruded itself into his pleasant dream country and disturbed its peace, he seems to have had constant access to his favourite dream places; the dreams that he relates are coherent and vivid, and moreover he has learnt the art that must be acquired if dream notes are to be of value, the art of full and accurate recording. But even if we are not so lucky as to have the right of entry into a favourite country every night at will, many of us have some place of dream into which from time to time we find our way; some dream house of which the key is ours. It is always with a certain glad surprise that we recognise rooms that have thus become familiar to us—passages every turn of which we know.

The construction of these dream houses, and the geography of dream places, are good examples of the methods of the dream mind, and of its curious way of handling and altering the memories of which it makes use in the building of dreams. Memory seems by choice to go back for the materials of these dream scenes to a more or less distant past; our actual surroundings at the present moment, the rooms, the streets, the countryside in which we are living, do not occur nearly as often as do the rooms and scenes of past years. In these, as in all its operations, the dream mind seizes upon memories that had almost faded from waking consciousness, and vividly renews them. In much the same way a photograph of a house, faintly remembered, brings back a thousand details which had grown dim in our minds, so that, having looked at it, we almost forget how much we had forgotten.

Of such dream memories of childhood de Quincey wrote: "The minutest incidents of childhood or forgotten scenes of later years were often revived. I could not be said to recollect them, for if I had been told of them when waking I should not have been able to acknowledge them as parts of my past experience. But placed as they were before me, in dreams like intuitions, and clothed in all their evanescent circumstances and accompanying feelings, I recognised them instantaneously."[1]

But the dream mind, though it depends upon the materials that memory supplies, hardly ever uses those materials without altering them. It would seem as though the dream imagination cannot rest satisfied simply with re-creating; it must build anew, it must alter, it must add. It will, for instance, select for the dream scene one floor only of a familiar house, or make choice of one remembered room, and will work this into another building, all else being omitted or changed. Or again, one particular garden corner will be used, and the rest neglected by this capricious artist. Just as the dream mind alters the meaning of a sound or other sense impression that reaches the brain, and as it changes the characters of a book that we are reading, so it transforms our recollections of familiar places, and pieces differ-

[1] De Quincey, "Confessions of an English Opium Eater."

ent pictures together in curious and unexpected combinations.

There is a house that I know well in my dreams, in which passages and stairways innumerable lead from attic to attic on many levels. Their floors are old and uneven; the walls are covered with a paper made long ago to resemble blocks of grey granite; I suppose it would be thought hideous nowadays, but in the dream house it seems to me wholly delightful, for it has the charm of memory, the restfulness of something very familiar. When I try to trace the geography of the dream house, I recognise the real attics and passages from which it took its origin. With a thousand other memories the dream house has grown out of the old country home of my childhood. The attics have changed places, rooms belonging to another house have got built into the dream house. In many ways it is altered, but things that matter remain unchanged. I know the very smell of the store-cupboard round the next corner, where the damson cheese and jellies in tiny leaf-shaped moulds are stored. I know that in the further attic the scent of jasmine will come in at the casement window, and the jasmine sprays will tap lightly against the panes just as they used to do; and at the end of the passage wooden steps, worn unevenly into hollows, will lead down into a warm and friendly kitchen. The literal faithfulness of many of the details recalled in these dreams is as characteristic of the dream mind as the capriciousness with which it makes its selections amongst our memories, which must all, it seems, be transmuted by the alchemy of the imagination.

De Quincey's dream of Easter is as perfect an illustration as could be found of such alterations made in a dream scene, and of the blending of memories of places that are far apart into one dream picture. This beautiful dream, moreover, has little of the strangeness, and none of the horror, that characterised many of those that he recorded, and that made his nights so full of agitation and misery.

"I thought it was a Sunday morning in May, that it was Easter Sunday, and as yet very early in the morning. I was standing, as it seemed to me, at the door of my own cottage. Right before me lay the very scene which could be commanded from that situation, but exalted, as was usual, and solemnised by the power of dreams. There were the same mountains, and the same lovely valley at their feet; but the mountains were raised to more than Alpine height, and there was interspace far larger between them of meadows and forest lawns. . . . I gazed upon the well-known scene, and I said aloud (as I thought) to myself, 'It wants yet much of sunrise; and it is Easter Sunday; and that is the day on which they celebrate the first-fruits of resurrection. I will walk abroad; old griefs shall be forgotten to-day; for the air is cool and still   with the dew I can wash the fever from my forehead, and then I shall be unhappy no longer.' And I turned, as if to open my garden gate; and immediately I saw upon the left a scene far different; but which the power of dreams had reconciled into harmony with the other. The scene was an Oriental one; and there also it was Easter Sunday, and very early in the morning. And at a vast distance were visible, as a stain upon the horizon, the domes and cupolas of a great city—an image or faint abstraction, caught perhaps in childhood from some picture of Jerusalem. And now a bow-shot from me, upon a stone and shaded by Judean palms, there sat a woman; and I looked; and it was—Ann." [1]

In the little book that has already been quoted, Mr. Martin speaks of the sense of pleasure renewed with which he enters his dream country, and, like him, I find it difficult to describe how happy some of these dreams are. When I have waked from them and have begun to write them down, I have wondered why it should seem so hard to be torn away from them, when so little had happened, and why they should give such an odd unexplained sense of joy. Dreams, so uneventful that it seems hardly worth while to record them at all, will give us that delicious childish sense of happiness. It is childlike, and that is no doubt in great part the secret of our pleasure. In dreams the responsibility that rests upon us by day is taken from us. Only the things of the present moment matter; and in this respect we become like children. I am sure that we "Olympians" make far too much of the actual happiness of the state of childhood; it is often infinitely happier to be "grown up"; but in this respect at least childhood is for-

2 De Quincey, "Confessions."

tunate, and we, in our good dreams, are fortunate too; the weight of responsible care is for a little while lifted from us. It is because when we leave the dream country we leave that happy state of irresponsibility behind us that we feel such a pang of regret when we have to turn aside and come back to a workaday world where we have once more to shoulder our natural duties and cares. For a little while we had forgotten them and they were laid aside, but now again our lives belong not to ourselves but to others, and we often take up life again with a chill sense of disappointment. We come back, it is true, to a world that is just as lovely to look upon as the dream world that we have left, but we ourselves are different, and the spell is broken. In one of the most perfect of his essays, Elia tells his dream children of the great house in Norfolk, presided over by their great-grandmother Field, telling them "how I could never be tired with roaming about that huge mansion with its vast empty rooms, with their worn-out hangings, fluttering tapestry, and carved oaken panels, with the gilding almost rubbed out." When we read afresh the tender wistful words with which Elia's story of his dream children closes, they bring back to us the same forlorn sense of disappointment that we also feel when we are called away from our happy dreams. We too are rueful to leave a dream country where we would so gladly have lingered. Elia's beautiful dream house, with its stately walled gardens, was built up from the faithful memories of his childhood, just as are the dream houses to which we go back oftenest in our sleep. But there are other dreams in which we discover and explore buildings that are quite unlike these familiar places, and unlike anything that we have ever known by day. I am not thinking of the creations of fevered dreams, or of such monstrous inventions of drugged sleep as some of those described by de Quincey, but only of things that we may meet with in the course of ordinary dreams of healthy sleep. In some of these ordinary dreams imagination forsakes altogether the familiar lines of the architecture that we are accustomed to, and boldly creates for itself original buildings that seem to the dreamer at least to be new and noble in design. A museum, vast and splendid, with reading-rooms and stately galleries, and a new national picture gallery with great entrance doors, that open wide above broad curving flights of steps rising from a street thronged with traffic, have become familiar places in my dreams. Their lofty corridors and great staircases and doorways seem to be constructed as many dream buildings are, for us to fly in, rather than to walk in. They seem also to have a gayer atmosphere than that of our real museums, and as I have entered their doors I have said to myself, "I remember this pleasant place—I know that here I shall be happy."

All of us who know a particular dream country well, know the delight with which we recognise some especial characteristic landmark that has come to have associations of its own for us in this dream world. I do not know how far a great story-teller needs to experience the sensations that he writes of; in the "Brushwood Boy," Mr. Kipling has described with the wonderful air of truth that he is master of, the emotion of pleasure that such recognition brings, and also the curious way in which certain elements of a dream will persist for years in our dreams until they may even become factors of importance in our waking as well as in our sleeping hours. No doubt others have had experiences similar to those of the boy who constantly "found himself sliding into dreamland by the same road—a road that ran along a beach near a pile of brushwood. To the right ran the sea, sometimes at full tide, sometimes withdrawn to the very horizon; but he knew it for the same sea. By that road he would travel over a swell of rising ground covered with short withered grass, into valleys of wonder and unreason." [1] The boy in this story was not singular in having a definite dream spot which came to be the "jumping-off" place for all his best dreams. Many dreamers find that they have some such starting-place, and indeed Mr. Kipling's story would not seem as convincing as it does if it were simply a fanciful creation, unrelated to real experiences shared by other dream adventurers.

Many years ago a friend gave me the following account of a recurrent place dream which seems to have affected not only her dream life but also her normal waking life. "You know," she wrote, "that I live in sight of a wide plain stretching away to very

[1] Rudyard Kipling, "A Day's Work."

distant hills. The plain is always changing with
changing lights and shadows. You can watch it best
from certain high open places where the woods end
and the uplands begin. A path through the woods
comes out on to one of these open places. Standing
there you look out over the wide distance of the plain,
east and west and north. Long ago I found that this
particular spot with this view of the plain came constantly into my dreams. They had a way of forming
round it. The dreams varied very much, but I noticed that all those that I liked best—the dreams that
led to fine adventures—began there. By degrees I
came to feel that just as the happiest dreams started
in that place, anything supremely good that might
come into my life, and the greatest of its adventures,
would surely begin there, too.

"The place of dreams gradually became a curious
sort of touchstone for the people who came about me
and who cared for me. 'I shall not,' I said to myself in the rashness of my confident youth, 'marry
anyone who does not find his own way to the dream
place, and understand its significance.' I should not
be writing this to you if my dream story had ended
differently. When after months of separation . . .
came, and led me straight to the dream place, without word or sign from me, I knew that my dreams
had been true in their foreshadowing, and that they
were now at last to be perfectly fulfilled."

This account was given by my friend as an instance
of what she regarded as a series of prophetic dreams.
It may be so, but it seems to me rather an instance

of the strong influence that a recurrent place dream may have even upon our waking mind.   The effect of a dream which persists in this way, and which repeats itself as an echo does, becomes intensified by the fact of repetition.   The series of dreams which extended over many months had evidently strongly affected my friend's waking and sleeping thoughts. Thought-reading of a simple kind such as was here involved would be no difficult matter to the insight of love; love and comprehension went hand in hand in her lover's case, and I think that his intuitive perception of the trend of her thoughts led him without difficulty to her place of dreams.

CHAPTER IX

DREAM CONSTRUCTION

O magic sleep! O comfortable bird!
That broodest o'er the troubled sea of the mind
Till it is hush'd and smooth! O unconfined
   Restraint! imprisoned liberty! great Key
   To golden palaces, strange mintrelsy,
Fountains grotesque, new trees, bespangled caves,
Echoing grottoes, full of trembling waves
And moonlight; ay, to all the mazy world
Of silvery enchantment!

              —KEATS, *Endymion.*

When we try to define the essential difference between our thoughts and our dreams, the greater incoherence of dreams will probably most often be suggested. I do not myself hold the belief that in consecutiveness and incoherence are particularly characteristic of dreaming; certainly not that they are essential to it. They are often associated in our minds with the dream state, but chiefly because our memory of dreaming is so imperfect that links of thought which are necessary to make the memory of a dream coherent are often forgotten when we wake. It is these links of thought that make a rational connection between the successive stages of dream ideas, and that suggest various dream adventures that seem to be almost lunatic if these links in the chain are lost. A better system of dream memory would often remedy this, and would show us how orderly and, in a way, how rational are the methods of dream construction. Even by day, if we allow our thoughts to wander for a time at will, and then try to retrace all the byways that they followed, there will probably be some steps that we cannot recall. This is still more likely to be true in the case of dream consciousness, but the habit of retracing the steps of thought can be acquired as well with regard to our dreams as with regard to the course of our wandering thoughts by day.

I believe that in reality the essential difference between thinking and dreaming lies rather in the greater intensity with which imagination works in the dream state. A stray thought which comes into our mind by day is glanced at, is turned over, as it were, in our mind, and dismissed; and a hundred such thoughts may occur and be considered, without seriously deflecting the direction of the main current of our thought. But in a dream the process is different. When an idea comes to the surface of dream consciousness, the imagination seizes upon it, and not only looks at it but proceeds to embody it into a solid fact; it thus ceases to be simply an idea, and becomes a definite figure in three dimensions—a thing active and gifted with life. This power exercised by the dream imagination alters all the sequence of dreams and makes their course essentially different from that followed by our thoughts by day. This characteristic of dreams is exemplified in the following notes on dream construction, and these notes show also some of the links which connect together and explain the successive stages of a dream. It will be seen how without the memory of these links the dream falls to pieces and would appear quite incoherent to the waking mind.

"It was a winter's day, and I was looking at the gaily dressed windows of a shop in Oxford Street; its windows, filled with the little orange-trees and flowers of the Mayfair Flower Workers, attracted me and I stayed admiring them, jostled a little by the crowd of people who were continually passing by. The roadway also was thronged with motors and with motor omnibuses and—drawn up near the pavement where I stood I noticed more particularly —a small old-fashioned brougham that was painted dark blue, and that was drawn by a white horse. The next thing that I remember is that my attention was attracted upwards, and I remained for some time spell-bound, watching the curious, rather uncertain, flight of a dragon—a dragon with very short red wings, who was pulling an aerial car at some little height above the rest of the traffic and some way above the heads of the people in the crowded street. 'The dragon isn't nearly strong enough for the car he has got to pull,' I exclaimed; 'his wings are absurd little things, not nearly big enough for the job—why, a good aeroplane would be better than that!' The dragon was certainly rather feeble, but it kept up its jerky flight bravely along Oxford Street, and finally turned down Regent Street, where I lost sight of it."

Now, when I woke up later from this dream I could

see no mental link at all between the ordinary sights of the London street that I had been watching and the dragon car. But as I looked back more carefully at the picture film of memory I recalled the white horse that I had noticed just before the coming of the dragon, and that white horse was the clue that I sought. To those who dwell in our countryside the link connecting the thought of a white horse with the thought of a dragon is not far to seek. The original "White Horse" of King Alfred, scrawled upon the steep bluff of the Down that overlooks the Vale to which the White Horse gives its name, is indeed not a horse but a dragon shape—a white dragon drawn just as a prehistoric man or child might have drawn it; and carved in the soft turf of the Down it has survived the centuries unchanged. Now it often happens that in the old house under the Wiltshire Downs where this dream was dreamed, my eyes rest on certain little red and blue dragons who sprawl in engaging puppy-like attitudes on the covers and sides of the old Chinese dishes on my mantelpiece. From these funny dragon puppies with their wide mouths, their innocent kitten-like claws and feeble beginnings of wings, my thoughts have wandered away to other fiercer dragon shapes and dragon stories, to dragon-helmed warriors who came in dragon-keeled ships to our shores, or to Alfred's great Dragon Horse on the Downs.

The dragon of my dreams had the building wings of these baby dragons, absurdly inadequate for a beast of burden, but I have no doubt that from them the dream sprang, and that without them and without the White Horse the dream would have been dreamed quite differently. The building up of many of our long and elaborate dreams comes from such complete visualisation as this of each successive idea as it occurs.

Other steps in the process of dream construction are shown in the following note. The simplest type of dream is given here because it exemplifies better than one of more imaginative interest would do the actual building up of a dream.

"We were walking in a country unknown to me. We had crossed some grasslands and came to a roughly made stile of wooden bars, over which I helped my mother to climb. The path which we followed led down the side of a grassy slope which formed the side of a shallow winding valley. On our left the valley disappeared round a corner behind low hills. To our right a small foreign-looking village lay at a distance, too far off for us to see it clearly. Looking down the valley that we were descending into, I saw that the path lay across it like a white ribbon and then turned off to the right towards the distant village. 'It looks just like a road marked out upon a map,' I thought, 'or like a railway map.' As I looked again I saw that there was running down the length of the valley a railroad track which I had not seen before and which crossed the path that we were following. We came nearer, and I saw that no gates guarded the crossing of the roads. 'What a dangerous sort of level crossing,' I thought,

'like some of those unguarded railway lines in
America that we read of. There would be no warning whatever of a train coming from behind the
hills except the sound of it.' I listened, and then I
began to hear, far away, the roar of a train; it came
round the hill and round a sudden sharp curve at the
foot of the valley, rushing towards us very fast. I
stood clear of the line and watched it come and go.
'Will it stop at the village?' I wondered. As it
thundered by, three carriages at the end of the train
detached themselves from it and followed, but at a
lessening pace. 'Slip carriages for the village, of
course,' I thought. 'What a fine thing it is to see the
oncoming of a great train—it is like the description
of a stampede of wild cattle on the Western Plains.
These slip carriages are like the animals selected and
cut off by the herdsmen from the main body.'
Again the suggested thought realised itself at once.
From far down the valley there came the sound of
many hoofs beating the earth all together with a
deep sound, and there came tearing up it a vast body
of splendid wild cattle; their heads lowered, tossing
their horns. They came rushing up—they were not
very close to me, but I could see them part a little,
and a few young ones, who were trailing rather behind them, got separated and were left a short way
behind the rest.

"No sense of fear was in my mind and no great
surprise, 'I suppose that in this country it is natural
to see such great herds,' was my thought." The
dream after this followed on a tranquil course, and

nothing else occurred that needs to be recorded.

It is given here because it illustrates the process that constantly takes place in the making of a dream.

The winding path that we look down upon suggests the marking of roads and railroads on a map; the railroad idea having been thus suggested, the dream mind seizes on it and makes it objective, and the railway at once takes its place in the dream valley. Path and railroad cross each other, and the crossing suggests the next step in the story. A rapid sequence of ideas flashes through the mind somewhat as follows: a level crossing—its possible dangers—stories of accidents in certain American states at level crossings—sound of the train the only warning. Just such a sequence of thoughts as might occur if we were glancing at such a scene by day. But no sooner has the thought of the warning noise of a train flashed into the dream mind than it seizes upon this particular idea, and converts it into an actual fact. In the dream we listen, and in a few seconds the sound is heard. Imagination and memory work together so well that a perfect realisation of the roar of a train, increasing in sound as the train comes from behind the hills is produced. The illusion is complete.

The dream goes on. I watch the foreshortened train as it rushes towards me, and the rush suggests the image of a charge of wild cattle. This image links on to the idea of the Western States just now recalled to mind, and suggests a ranch, and the ranchmen skilfully separating the required number of ani-

mals from the herd.   The simile is worked out rather
fancifully by the dream imagination, in obedience to
which the slip carriages are detached from the train.
Then the imagination visualises the actual herd.   It
sees them come from afar; it hears—or makes me
hear—the very sound of their trampling feet.

Now this elaborate process of dream building is
very much like the process that is carried on in the
mind by day when images pass quickly across it,
and one association calls up another.   Only at night
the imagination is not fettered by the discipline
which restrains our wandering thoughts from following too eagerly in the random track of every
chance thought and suggestion.   The imagination in
sleep, unchecked in this way, can devote itself to perfecting each successive image that arises, giving life
and reality to each of them in turn, metamorphosing
them, and constantly adding new facts and fresh
touches to the pictures which are its creation.

This simple explanation of the method of construction of one very ordinary type of dream will seem
quite inadequate to those who believe that the origin
and contents of dreams are to be explained only on
the basis of Freudian psycho-analysis.   The theory
of dream building by the association of ideas which
seems to account for the making of many of these
dreams does not take into consideration the symbolisms and hidden meanings that the psycho-analyst
finds in all of them.   I do not question that there
may be dreams that may symbolise the repressed
or unconscious wish of Freudian teaching; others no

doubt have a symbolic character, and represent some thought or mood experienced by the dreamer. But beside these, there are numberless dreams which do not seem to belong to either of these categories; the construction of some of these may be accounted for by the theory of associated ideas. No single theory seems capable of explaining every kind of dream, and when we try to reason about dreams we have to take refuge once more in the fact that they are not all alike, but are so manifold in their nature as are the thoughts and imaginations of men.

CHAPTER X

A dream itself is but a shadow.—HAMLET, *ii, 2.*

In the numerous scientific books written about dreams a classification has been generally adopted dividing them into presentative (or sensorial) dreams, originating in physical impressions made upon the dreamer, and representative (or psychic) dreams, which originate in his mental impressions and in the memories which float up from the reserves of the brain; but the distinction thus made seems to be only a partially true one, for dreams do not actually fall thus into two perfectly separate groups. It would probably be nearer the truth to say that whereas all our dreams are made up of mental impressions and woven out of memories, sensory impressions and vibrations, starting either from within the body or from outside it, serve often to evoke those memories and to call up the mental images that dreams are composed of.

The dream consciousness tries to account for every sensory impression that it feels, and in order to do this it invents a coherent and plausible explanation which it proceeds to weave into a dream story. It is always difficult to know to what extent the dream consciousness is stimulated in this way by sensory impressions, because, apart from the nature and occurrences of the dream itself, it is generally impossible when we wake up to tell what sensations or vibrations played a part in and influenced the dream consciousness while we slept; whether, for instance, during our sleep a little noise occurred which may have suggested an incident in the dream, or whether some slight sense of bodily discomfort such as undue warmth or cold may have altered its current. In most cases we can only make a vague guess at the nature of these sense impressions, for the dream mind transforms the sound or other slightly disturbing sensation into something wholly different from the original physical cause. A piece of wood falls lightly on the hearth while we sleep; the dream consciousness does not recognise the sound for what it actually is, but may imagine it to be the crash of an avalanche or transform it into the sound of far-off guns; a wasp buzzes against the window-pane and the dream consciousness turns it into the drone of an aeroplane, and will forthwith develop the dream round the incident that is thus suggested. Parables and symbols are the language and the means of expression of the dream consciousness, but we are often unable to recognise or to interpret the meaning of the fable that has thus been constructed. As Mr. Havelock Ellis has expressed it—whatever the physical cause may have been that has started the dream consciousness into activity—"the internal and external stimuli which act upon sleeping consciousness are not a part of that consciousness, nor in any real sense its source or its cause. The ray of sunlight that falls on the dreamer, the falling off of his bed-clothes, the indigestible supper he ate last night—these things can no more 'account' for his dream than the postman's knock can account for the contents of the letter he delivers. Whatever the stimuli from the physical world that may knock at the door of dreaming consciousness, that consciousness is apart from them, and stimuli can only reach it by undergoing transformation. They must put off the character they wear as phenomena of the waking world, they must put on the character of phenomena of another world, the world of dreams.''

The following is an example of a transformation of this kind:

I had been thinking intently for a long time before I slept of the anxieties of a friend who was engaged in a difficult task of nursing. A sudden spell of cold brought on some slight rheumatic pain during the night, of which I had not been conscious before I went to sleep. The pain came into my dream but was transferred to my friend. In it she became the patient—I was helping to nurse her, and my mind was concentrated on the problems and practical difficulties that she and I had lately discussed; the pain, which was really my own, being one of the symptoms of the illness that she was suffering from in the dream.

This sensation was clearly one of the elements that entered into the construction of this dream, but it was only one element, for the thoughts that had filled my mind during the day and had preoccupied me before I slept gave the dream its shape and suggested practically all its incidents. Both sensation and memory alike underwent a dream change—they were transformed—and assumed, as Mr. Ellis has explained, the character of phenomena of the world of dreams:

It is certain that many dreams are thus stimulated by sensory impressions, often probably very slight ones which are never wholly extinguished during sleep; and if we could retrace our dreams more perfectly we should frequently find that incidents composing them originated in such a way as has been described. But dreams are of infinite variety, and I am convinced that there are also many that owe their existence to the action of memory alone, and that they are carried through by the dream mind without there having necessarily been any external stimulus or sense impression to account for them.

Amongst dreams that we find most often quoted as being initiated by physical causes are our dreams of flight. We are told by most writers on dreams that these are certainly due to sense impressions, and it is generally assumed that the sense of flying or floating is caused by the fact that in sleep our feet are not resting on the ground, that they miss the accustomed sense of the earth's resistance, and that the subconscious mind in the exercise of its reasoning faculty comes to the conclusion that this unfamiliar absence of pressure signifies a condition in which the body must be floating in mid-air. This may be the true cause of many flying dreams, but as far as I can judge from the series of experiments which I have made, it is not a satisfactory explanation of my own dreams of flying. This particular type of dream was chosen as one to be watched and recorded, and from these experiments it seems to me that sense impressions do not influence these dreams nearly as certainly and powerfully as mental impressions influence them. I have already described how, by concentrating the mind upon the subject, these dreams can be made to recur, and how the accomplishment of definite acts of flight and new methods of flying can be acquired by the exercise of will-power.

On the other hand, I have made very many attempts to see whether some particular bodily attitude during sleep would have any effect upon dream flying. My notes show that lying on my back, lying upon either side, or as I often lie face downwards with my head pillowed on one arm, the sleeping attitude apparently makes no difference whatever to the flying dream. I made other experiments to see whether a pillow wedged at the foot of the bed, so that the feet were firmly pressed against it, would make any difference, but it did not apparently do so. The hands, moreover, are constantly used in these dreams, a slight waving or paddling motion giving direction or velocity to the flight; but I find that I fly just as well if either or both my hands are imprisoned under the body, and even the fact of waking up with one hand "gone to sleep" by reason of continued pressure on it has not apparently affected the dream.

The conclusion that I gather from these experiments is that, whilst by an act of will it is possible to recapture the flying dream, and whilst the memory of past acts of flight helps to make such dreams recur, I can find little confirmation of the theory that these particular dreams are caused by physical sensations. The question of dream control has, however, been fully discussed and only belongs very indirectly to the question now under consideration of the part that sensory impressions play in the causation of our dreams.

Having read of experiments being made to test whether dreams are directly affected by the senses of smell and taste, I tried certain of these experiments, and for this purpose kept on my pillow at night a few lavender flowers or rose-leaves, or a tiny grain of camphor or spice; but whilst the presence of one of these scented things leaves my dreams untouched, it will produce a most vivid impression in the moments between sleeping and waking. This intensification of the senses when sleep is approaching has probably often been observed. The subject belongs more properly to a later chapter. Here I need only say that whilst at these times the senses of smell and taste become abnormally acute, these sense impressions do not ''carry on'' into the dreams that follow, and do not apparently influence them in any way. Incidents often occur in dreams in which I enjoy something that has a delicious flavour, but these incidents seem always to spring from memories of taste, and can be traced back to such memories, but not to any actual or present sensation; for even when a morsel of spice has been kept in the mouth during sleep it has not succeeded in affecting the dream.

The sense of warmth and cold seems to affect dreaming more than any other direct sense impression, and both the nature of dreams and the power of remembering and recording them are influenced by the degrees of bodily warmth during sleep.

It is a fact for which there is probably some quite simple physical explanation, that in order to be able to recall long dreams easily and accurately the body must be kept fairly and evenly warm; and as I personally like to sleep under only very light coverings, I have learned that I must add to these if the best dreams are to be dreamed or recorded. Delightful dreams are more apt to recur, and are more apt to be vivid in character, if the body is kept fairly warm during sleep. On the other hand, many people bear testimony to the fact that sleeping under an eiderdown quilt or any coverings that produce undue warmth "give bad dreams" to the sleeper. I do not know of any other purely physical means by which the nature of dreams can be thus easily altered, but by variations in bodily temperature I have found that they can be modified, and the recording of long and complicated dreams is made easier to me if that temperature is rather carefully regulated.

From whatever side we approach the subject of dreams there seems to be endless variety in individual experience concerning them, and on no point do dreamers seem to differ more widely than as to the memory that they retain in dreams of sense impressions.

To those who have a very complete and full dream life, and for whom these experiences make up no inconsiderable part of the pleasure of living, all sense impressions will naturally take their due place during sleep. The memory of colour, light, and sound, of fine taste and delicate scent, and all the delight that our keenest sense impressions give us, should naturally be found repeating themselves in dreams; but in this respect, as in so many others, there is a surprising diversity in people's experiences. It is interesting to note the answers that we get if we put such questions to our friends as: "Do you see colour in your dreams? Is your dream world of varied colour like our own, or is it neutral tinted?" Although, I suppose, we all spend a considerable proportion of our life in dreaming, it is curious to find how many people, when they are asked such a question, cannot answer it, or recall with clearness anything about these aspects of their dream life. Some people, however, have told me at once that either they see no colour at all in dreams or that colour has made so little impression on them that they have no recollection of it. A few have said that their dream world is definitely colourless like a monochrome drawing, and that there seems to be very little bright sunlight or deep shadow in it. Others, again, say, and say most convincingly, that they see everything with the colours, lights, and shadows that we see in the world of day; but perhaps the commonest experience is to be able to recall very clearly some one passage or note of colour in a dream, whilst all recollection of colour in the rest of it has passed away. In nearly all my own dreams I find this to be the case; the one colour note that is recalled is generally vividly retained, but the other objects of the dream are not remembered in colour at all, colour not being the fact about them that has arrested the attention enough to be remembered.

When in after years I read in Robert Louis Stevenson's "Chapter on Dreams" that as a child he had been "haunted by nothing more definite than a certain hue of brown," which he did not mind in the least when he was awake, but feared and loathed while he was dreaming, it recalled vividly a dream which used from time to time to haunt my own childhood. At a spot in Kensington Gardens which is now dominated by Watts' statue of "Physical Energy," the dream used to begin. The slow ticking of a watch gave warning, but alas! too late, of what was inevitably approaching. In the eastern sky a cloud would come slowly sailing up till it reached and covered the zenith, a cloud of a shade of purplish brown which for some unknown reason was dreadful to me, and lastly, from somewhere very far away there would come the sound of the roll of drums. I thought life could hold nothing more full of fear than that colour accompanied by that distant sound, and no daylight reasoning gave me reassurance, until by a happy chance I learned how to make my escape from all such haunting dreams.

A statement that appeared some years ago in a medical journal to the effect that colour vision in dreams is more often than not either imperfect or altogether absent, suggested this point to me as one that might well be noticed and recorded. I showed my notes to my father and asked him about his own memory of colour.

He said that colour was always a prominent thing in his dreams. He instanced one favourite dream that from an early age had recurred from time to time during his long life. In it he would find himself on the top of the stage-coach, on which as a little boy he used to travel part of the lengthy journey between his school and his home, but the dream journey took him through country unknown to him, and of singular beauty. He described the gradual descent of the coach into a wide and fair valley; the colour of the trees on either side and the exquisite blue of the far distance that could be seen beyond the furthest limits of the valley were the elements in the dream scene that had made the greatest impression on his memory. The subject having been thus suggested, he told me of other dreams in which colour vision was a prominent feature. Colour sense was evidently strong in them, and often seemed to be the point that most impressed his memory. The blossoming and vivid colour of his favourite crimson hawthorn-tree in a dream was reported to me one May morning during the last week of his life. My mother's dreams also seem to centre round colour, and colour seems to be the fact in them that she remembers most clearly.

"In a gentian dream last night," she records, "I found a lovely clump of *Gentiana verna* growing on low rocks together with a mossy-looking plant whose yellower green was in strong contrast with the colour of the leaves of the gentian—the starry flowers were, of course, of the deep gentian blue."

Just as some people describe their dream world as being a colourless one, others say that they have no sense of smell in their dreams.[1] Possibly it is their memory of these sense impressions that is at fault, for I find in my own notes many observations of smell as well as of taste, observations not only of fragrant flower scents, but also of subtler impressions of smell such as that which occurs in the following dream: "I was motoring through a countryside of steep hills and valleys; dusk was beginning to fall; 'lighting-up time' had not actually come, but I was warned by the faint scent, cold, clean and unmistakable, that belongs to valley mist, that, besides the natural darkening of the evening, a light mist was beginning to rise and to obscure the road."

The sense of taste comes also into certain dreams, but all these impressions are quickly forgotten when we wake. I have looked at the wares of many a

[1] "Very infrequently do we dream words, and almost never do we dream smells or tastes."—Lay, "Man's Unconscious Conflict," p. 167.

confectioner, in the hope, never, I fear, to be realised in a waking world, that I might find amongst them the candy of a certain dream, candy of an entrancing green colour, and of a flavour that only a dream confectioner seems able to supply.

CHAPTER XI

Some say that gleams of a remoter world visit the soul in sleep.

—SHELLEY, *Mont Blanc*.

"There is reason to suppose that our normal consciousness represents no more than a *slice* of our whole being. We all know that there exist *sub*conscious and *un*conscious operations of many kinds both organic, as secretion, circulation, etc., which are in a sense below the operations to which our minds attend; and also our mental, as the recall of names, the development of ideas, etc., which are on much the same level as the operations to which our minds attend, but which for various reasons remain in the background of our mental prospects. Well, besides these subconscious and unconscious operations, I believe that *super-conscious* operations are also going on within us; operations, that is to say, which transcend the limitations of ordinary faculties of cognition, and which yet remain—not *below the threshold* —but rather *above the upper horizon* of consciousness, and illumine our normal experience only in transient and cloudy gleams."[1]

No roads of enquiry offer greater inducements to

[1] F. Myers, A Note in "Phantasms of the Living," vol. ii, p. 285.

the explorer of dream problems than those leading to the study of the transition stage which lies between sleeping and waking. I have travelled only a short way along these roads, and have been able to do little more than observe their beginnings and their direction.

Widely varying stages of consciousness are included within this borderland state. It embraces experiences which stand in so close a relationship to our dreams that no clearly defined boundary can be drawn between them; and on the other hand we meet from time to time within its borders with experiences far removed from dreams, apparently unrelated to our dream life, and which have a very special character of their own.

The process of going to sleep may conveniently be divided into two stages, although no clearly marked division does in fact separate them. The earlier stage, further removed from sleep, is the state of quiet, when the body being soothed and tranquillised, restlessness ceases, when impressions from without need disturb us little, when thought can still be concentrated and directed inwards, and our attention is still under our control. The later stage is the state of semi-consciousness that shades off imperceptibly into sleep, when concentration begins to lessen, attention wanders, and we cease to direct the mind's flight, until finally borderland consciousness gives place to dream consciousness.

I propose to deal first with the earlier stage, the state of tranquillity. At the beginning of this book the question was asked, "Does any faculty of the mind change its character and assume functions different from those which it possesses normally?" I believe that such a change does take place in both stages of the borderland state. In the earlier state of tranquillity certain mental faculties appear to operate with heightened powers; and, as will be seen later, in the stage verging on sleep the same phenomenon may be observed in the case of certain faculties of sense.

In that earlier state of quiet, when the activity of the body is stilled, we are able with the help of darkness to exclude irrelevant visual impressions, and to arrive at a certain measure of freedom from extraneous thoughts. In this condition we may suddenly find that the mind is working in a manner different from that which is normally characteristic of it. At such moments the answer to some difficult question, which has intrigued us and baffled our intelligence by day, may flash into the mind, appearing to come to us from without rather than from within. The missing links of thought that were needed have been supplied, we know not how; we are only aware that whereas something was previously lacking, the chain of thought is now entire, and the deduction drawn from it is complete. The process is similar to that which takes place in the "super-dream," but occurs on the hither side of the boundary of sleep instead of beyond it. In either case there is the same sense of surprise, when the answer comes, provided apparently by an agent or by a mental faculty which does not seem to work in the same way, or with the same limitations of power as our normal mind.

The following note is given as an illustration of such a borderland experience which closely resembles the working of a "super-dream": One of the problems about dreams that this book is concerned with had been occupying my thoughts for some time. I had found it very puzzling, and I made no progress with the chapter that I was attempting to write. One night I had passed into the stage of borderland quiet, and should presently have travelled on to the state of sleep; my passage to the dream world was, however, interrupted by the intrusion of a recurrent word or thought. Without any effort of will on my part the thought proceeded to shape itself. I can only describe my relation to this process as being that of a spectator watching it. From being first a word, and then a nebulous idea, it became more and more distinct until shortly after the argument seemed to be completed, but externally, so to speak, to myself. In order to get rid of the too insistent chain of reasoning, and to avoid the effort of remembering it, I took pencil and paper which lay near at hand and wrote it down. Once written, it was pushed into the drawer by my bedside, and I slept. During the following days and weeks I was wholly absorbed in other work and in the anxieties brought about by the war, and this record lay in the drawer completely forgotten. So easy is it to lose all recollection of experiences that occur near the border-line of sleep, that when, some three or four weeks later, I came upon the written sheets, and had deciphered the scribbled semi-shorthand writing, I was bewildered as to their origin. At first I thought that I had at some time copied them from a book, but they were evidently intended as an integral part of my own book and argument, and then the forgotten border-land experience came back to me and I remembered it all clearly. The argument which came to me in this way required no alterations; I agreed with its reasoning, but it still seems to me to be not quite "mine," and to be the expression of a mind more logical than my own.

This stage of the borderland state is peculiar not only by reason of this heightening of the mental faculties, but also because it is the condition in which certain abnormal experiences are met with, which are among the most curious and significant of which the human mind is capable. The following note re-lates to such an abnormal experience which occurred to me while in this condition. It happened only once in my life; it seemed so different in nature from any-thing else that I had known and has remained so entirely outside all my ordinary experience that, although I now know that a similar thing has hap-pened to others, I shall have found it difficult to be-lieve in it, if it had not happened to myself.

I awoke before six o'clock one morning in my London bedroom and lay quietly thinking in a mood of great stillness. Quite suddenly my spirit seemed to leave my body—at least it is only in such words as these that I can describe what happened. I found myself outside my body—looking downwards from a little height above the foot of the bed at my own form lying there just below me. I saw O——, I saw my bed and the pale wall behind it, and the light window—I saw myself—but it was *I,* my own self, who looked on, who thought, and who in an instant was conscious of intolerable loneliness and of a great sense of desolation.

I wanted—how intensely I wanted—to come back to the warmth and shelter of human love! I felt that I could not bear the separation from everything I understood and loved—and I crept back shuddering into my bodily existence. I know that I was crying bitterly when I came back, and that it needed all the comfort that O—— could give me to make me feel safe again; because for a time I felt so insecurely anchored to life and to my body. By degrees the feeling of distress went away, and I was comforted when I realised how completely I had still been my own self whilst this happened; how unchanged my identity was during those moments when I was freed from my body and looked at it from the outside.

Such riddles of the mind as these are very puzzling when we meet them thus as isolated individual experiences; they fall into their proper place in such books as "Phantasms of the Living," where they are duly related to other similar phenomena of dream and border consciousness.

"The submerged life of the mind, however mysterious and elusive, yet persistently attracts the naturalist of the mental world."[1] The mystery and elusiveness of the mental phenomena which belong especially to the border state have always made a strong appeal to thinkers like Mr. Myers and those who have followed along similar paths of enquiry. They have not been afraid to acknowledge that many of these phenomena lie beyond man's present knowledge, and still elude his understanding. There is a readiness now to approach in a spirit of enquiry questions which would not formerly have been admitted as matters for serious study and discussion. Amongst such questions none has perhaps attracted more attention and exacted more controversy than that of the possible existence of a human faculty, hitherto unrecognised by science, by means of which communications may take place between mind and mind through channels other than those of the senses. This question of telepathic communication is being systematically examined from different points of view by many of the most serious thinkers of the present day, and all available evidence for and against the existence of such a faculty is being considered and weighed. Some among them, for instance Professor Lodge, men whose names are known and honoured throughout the world of science, go further, and affirm with unquestionable sincerity their assurance that such communications are not only transmitted from living mind to living mind, but are also transmitted by those who have crossed the threshold of death.

[1] Jastrow, "The Unconscious."

The implications of this belief are so great, involving as this faith does the vital question of man's survival of bodily death, that whilst it excites in many minds the most intense interest, it seems with equal force to repel others. The discussion of questions of such vast magnitude, which are the field of such acute controversy, is beyond the scope of this book; but these questions cannot be ignored when writing about the borderland state, for there is an intimate connection between them which must be taken into account when the nature of the mental faculties and the manner of their operation in this state are considered. All that can fittingly be urged is that, whatever view be taken, our judgment should not be formed without a study of the evidence that is available. This evidence is no longer left to mere hearsay; much has been collected and sifted by men of distinction in science, letters, and philosophy. Some of the evidence collected has been already published in the journals and Proceedings of the Society for Psychical Research, and have been dealt with in the writings of Sir Oliver Lodge, Mr. Myers, Mr. Gurney, and others. Much still remains to be published which will eventually be available. Evidence that has been tested in the "spirit of critical examination and enquiry" that these men have brought to bear on it cannot be lightly dismissed, even by those whose natural inclinations would lead them to reject any such investigation; it deserves at the least respectful and attentive study. But however scientifically such evidence as this has been weighed, however judicially tested, it is quite possible that it may never wholly satisfy men's natural longing for positive and easy certainties of proof. It will always be impossible to prove with the simple conclusiveness of a problem in geometry that certain of the mental experiences of which some of us may feel most sure, but which are outside the common run of men's experience, are indeed facts and not illusion.

From the very nature of these phenomena, no easy proof is possible, and the evidence concerning them cannot be grasped at all "without a mind sufficiently open to permit the beginning of an unusual course of study."[1] It will therefore never bring conviction to the large class of persons who have resolved that things that lie beyond their own experience, and outside the ordinary experience of men, are impossible and not to be believed. There are very many such persons, and for them these problems will remain questions that they consider it idle to discuss, and lying outside the province of possible or profitable knowledge. We may, however, remind ourselves that the boundaries which men have from time to time laid down as limits of human knowledge which mankind would do well not to try to overstep have varied with every successive age. To-day men are pushing forward along new roads and are opening up new regions of thought and experience of which the last century had little conception, and the limits of which we cannot see. But even though this is the case, and though the new regions of enquiry

1 Sir Oliver Lodge, letter to *The Times.*

be recognised as lawful fields for scientific investigation, there are still great difficulties in the way of obtaining the evidence that is required with regard to many experiences of the human mind. This is especially true of evidence of the transmission of messages from mind to mind when such communications are believed to come not from the living but from the dead. It is clear that much evidence will be required before this belief meets with general acceptance; at the same time, this evidence is especially difficult to obtain because these experiences are necessarily so intimate that they are seldom spoken of, but are treasured in the heart as things too near and too dear to be generally communicated. Their very nature often precludes their discussion, although they may be as convincing to the recipient of them as any other of the deepest experiences of the human spirit. If this were not the case, it would, I think, be found that these experiences are less rare than men have supposed. The dread of giving way to superstition or of being thought superstitious, the fear of possible self-deception, combined with our natural reluctance to speak of things that are so closely interwoven with our most intimate joys and sorrows, prevent our imparting to or learning from each other much that would be of the deepest interest and value.

Few of us have either the faith or the moral courage that made it possible to give to the world such a book as "Raymond"; for most of us the barriers in the way of such sincere revelation are too great, and hence our records will perhaps always be incomplete and scantier than they need otherwise be, but perhaps even this difficulty will not for ever stand in the way, when we realise more fully the need of this knowledge, and the necessity of testing and sifting the evidence that bears on it. Whatever our beliefs may be, whether we stand, as I certainly do, among those to whom the survival of human personality after bodily death, and the power of communication with those who have so survived, are realities and facts of experience, or whether we are in the large majority, for whom this faith in the possibility of communication between the living and the dead is at the utmost a matter of very doubtful conjecture, we may all agree that it is a question that transcends our understanding, and that in any case we stand only upon the threshold of such knowledge.

There are, however, other open points which, though they may also be disputable matters, excite less passionate and heated controversy. Amongst these are certain questions relating to possible telepathic communication between the living. If for the purposes of enquiry we may provisionally accept the hypothesis that under certain circumstances communications may take place between mind and mind through apparently immaterial channels, our enquiry might take the form of trying to ascertain whether either in the dream state or the borderland state the mind is specially sensitive to such impressions.

We cannot draw a hard and fast line between certain stages of borderland consciousness and the lightest stages of dreaming sleep, for the two states pass imperceptibly the one into the other. On the upper levels of sleep, when the dreamer is nearest to being awake, sense impressions from without have power more or less to affect his consciousness, and may alter the current of his dream. It may conceivably be the case that, in some such way as the senses of the dreamer are affected by sound or by light, a current of thought may influence a mind sensitive to such impressions. I have never found that in the actual dream state my own mind is specially gifted with this sensitiveness. The material and fashioning of dreams seem rather to come from within and to be the creation of my own mind; and although imagination working under dream conditions is marvellously quickened and heightened, it is generally occupied with the remembered facts of normal experience, facts which it alters and glorifies beyond recognition, but the materials of which are nevertheless supplied by memory. In other words, the greater number of dreams would seem to me to be evolved from without. On such points we each speak from our personal experience, and I can only say that in my own case my mind is not sensitive in this way in sleep.[1] In the course of all its dreaming activities it has never received with any conviction of certainty

[1] "Dreams form only a very subsidiary part of the evidence" (for telepathic communication); " . they do not prove telepathy; rather they are themselves shown to be telepathic by the analogies of the more cogent evidence drawn from waking hours . . . but they are instructive . . . they initiate us into the methods of subconscious processes."—Myers, "Phantasms of the Living."

the impression of messages or thoughts transmitted by another mind. Such messages I have received from time to time; but they have never come in dreams but always in the condition of partially suspended mental activity and complete bodily tranquillity attained in the quiet mood when we wait for sleep or have just emerged from it, when the normal activities of sensory perception are more or less in abeyance. Mr. Jastrow describes this state as "that state upon the verge of sleep in which the mind seems peculiarly open to suggestion"; and both my own and many other people's observations would seem to confirm the fact of this special receptiveness of the mind to suggestion and communication in the borderland state.

It is only in this state that I am personally familiar with the condition of tranquillity in which the mental faculties are thus heightened and sensitised; but I know that it is a state that is reached by others in other ways and at other times. Some are able to enter it when they choose by a definite act of will, by great concentration of mind, and by refusing to allow casual impressions to divert their attention. It is in such a condition that the inspiration of poets and thinkers, the spiritual vision of saints and mystics, has come to them. Their new conceptions, their clearest vision of spiritual things, have been realised in such moods. And it is in such moments, when the surface of the mind is unruffled like that of a dark still pool, that the artist finds himself able to apprehend a part of that essential truth that he is always seeking to express in his work.

The state in which at times the artist's mind works is, in fact, analogous in many respects to the mental condition reached in the borderland state. The following note that a painter sends me describing his own method of work, when the design of a picture is being thought out, is therefore not without interest in this place:

"At the crucial moment in the planning of a picture the design has to be fused into a unity; it is often necessary to shut oneself up alone, reduce the light, and bring the mind into a state of perfect stillness. The reduction of the light is of importance; not merely because the details of the design are thus subordinated, but because in darkness the mind is less disturbed by external stimuli, and becomes more receptive to the internal stimuli. It becomes easier to ignore the ascertained facts of a particular picture and to draw directly upon the imaginative memory which I suppose supplies one's dreams."

A somewhat similar state is described in the notebooks of Leonardo; and Kakki, the great Chinese painter of the eleventh century, gives a full description of the method by which he attained to this condition, which he found to be essential for his art.

"Ku K'ai-chih of Tsin builded a high-storied pavilion for his studio, that his thought might be more free. . . . Unless I dwell in a quiet house, seat myself in a retired room with the windows open, table dusted, incense burning, and the ten thousand trivial thoughts crushed out and sunk, I cannot have good feeling for painting or beautiful taste, and cannot create the 'yu' (the mysterious and wonderful)." [1]

The borderland state that we have been considering happens to present a certain analogy not only to the condition of mind in which the artist works, but also to the condition reached in hypnosis.

"When sleep is approaching, the flow of our thoughts is gradually diminished and the activity of the brain subsides; certain ideas and the neural systems corresponding to those ideas are still active.

There is still kept a certain channel of entry to the brain; and the impressions that are introduced at such a time tend to operate with abnormally great effect because they work in a free field, unchecked by rival ideas and tendencies." [2]

This brief extract from Mr. McDowell's account of hypnotic sleep and the approach to it describes a condition which obviously bears a strong resemblance to the approach of normal sleep; and Mr. McDowell's explanation of the manner in which cer tain impressions are enhanced suggests a possible explanation of the manner in which mental faculties are heightened in the transition state which we have described in this chapter.

This analogy is clearly one on which it would be

[1] Translation of an essay by Kakki. Fenellosa, "Epochs of Chinese and Japanese Art."

[2] W. McDowell, *Encyclopædia Britannica*, "Hypnotism."

dangerous for the amateur student, unequipped with the necessary scientific knowledge, to lay too much stress. Moreover, whilst the observations in this book are based upon personal experience, I have no such personal experience of the hypnotic state; any attempt to apply the suggested analogy would therefore almost certainly lead me into error.

CHAPTER XII

If the doors of perception were cleansed, everythirg would appear to man as it is, infinite. For man has closed himself up, till he sees all things through the narrow chinks of his cavern.—WILLIAM BLAKE.

The earlier stage of the borderland state has now been considered as far as my slender experience and knowledge enable me to discuss it, and we must now pass on to the later stage, that which is nearest to the verge of sleep. In the earlier stage the heightening of the mental faculties has been noted. I have made many notes on the similar phenomena which occur in the later stage of borderland consciousness; the curious heightening of sense impressions that take place when sleep is approaching. When we are nearest to sleep the senses become abnormally acute. A sudden apparent increase of the brightness of the light of a candle or lamp at these moments I find is very noticeable and in certain cases appears to act as a signal to the brain that the moment of crossing the border of sleep is at hand.

It would be interesting to compare with others our experience as to the increase in sensitiveness of the sense of smell. If a grain of something like spice or camphor be put under the pillow, or if a rose-leaf or two be left upon it, I find that scent will apparently intensify just before we sleep and when we wake. Three or four tiny grains from a spike of lavender will at such moments produce the effect of a concentrated lavender essence, and a scent so delicate that it would pass almost unperceived by day acquires at these times a powerful fragrance. We become, in fact, like the Princess in the fairy story who, when she lay down to sleep, was able to detect the presence of a pea hidden beneath the seven mattresses on which she rested. It might possibly be worth while to make more carefully planned and recorded experiments with regard to this heightened sensitiveness of the faculties of sight, hearing, and smell in this condition. That this special sensitiveness to these sense impressions does not in my own experience continue in the actual dream state has already been pointed out.[1] It affects us up to the moment when we come to the border of sleep, but in my experience it never crosses that border-line.

Of all our borderland experiences perhaps none are more attractive or more closely related to our dreams than the curious visions that sometimes present themselves to the mind when the will is in suspension, but whilst we are still more awake than asleep. These visions are so often referred to in books that they are evidently a common experience, although to different people they seem to come in very different forms, and with varying degrees of clearness and intensity. To me they come when, having been in bed, quietly resting for some little

[1] Chapter X, "Sense Impressions in Dreams."

time, my attention is arrested by seeing in front of me, as though between the rifts of a slowly unrolling cloud, a picture, which, as I watch it, changes and shifts. I believe that faces are often seen in this way, but the pictures that I see are seldom faces, they are generally landscape pictures with figures slowly moving across them. They represent places that I have never seen, although they are sometimes more or less like places that are known to me. These moving pictures dissolve and change, giving place to others which also come and go. They are apparently independent of any effort of imagination; their appearance is always rather a surprise, and I am totally unable to guess when or in what form they will come, or what the "picture on the screen" will change into.

The figures that are seen in these pictures move very slowly, and the effect is somewhat like the "dissolving views" which used to be shown at the "Polytechnic" when I was a child, combined with the movement of the cinematograph of to-day, but always as though it were seen through a gap in a curtain of misty cloud which is partly drawn aside. M. Maury, a French writer on dreams in the last century, wrote at some length about these visions, which he looked upon as actually part of the material from which our dreams are made, precursors of the dreams which fill the mind when we are quite asleep. The visions which he describes were generally of faces seen in the dark. Sir Francis Galton also described similar "visions of sane persons" experienced in the twilight time between sleeping and waking, having all the appearance of external objects, but which were not produced by any conscious effort of memory or imagination. Dream faces seem from most recorded accounts to be the objects that are the most frequently seen in these borderland visions.

Mr. Frederick Greenwood, in his book on dreams, describes vividly the faces that he was in the habit of seeing in this way: "Always of a distinctive character, these visionary faces are like none that can be remembered as seen in life or in pictures; indeed, one of their most constant and most remarkable characteristics is their amazing unlikeness . . . they strike the view as strangely strange, surprisingly original, and above all, intensely meaning" . . . "In all likelihood," he adds, "Blake's visions were some such phantoms as these, presented to his eyes in broad daylight." It should be noted that these borderland visions, whether of shifting land scapes or phantom faces, are wholly different in character and origin from the mental pictures which a trained memory enables us to call up by a definite act of will. The power of recalling scenes and visualising them is one of the best gifts that memory bestows on us, and few things give us greater pleasure than those recollections, which, like the poet's memory of daffodils, "flash upon the inward eye which is the bliss of solitude."

But borderland visions are far clearer and sharper than these; they are actually pictures which seem to be external to ourselves and which we *look at·* not pictures which are simply remembered. Moreover, it is the essential nature of these "visions" that no exertion of will can summon them at our pleasure, and that, as far as we can tell, they are wholly independent of our control, and not consciously dependent upon memory. Otherwise no special interest attaches to them, and apart from moments of pleasure that they give us they might not be worth even a passing reference, if it were not that they seem to be fashioned very much after the manner that dreams are fashioned, and apparently come from the same source as that which provides the materials and pictures of our dreams.

Another problem which might well be examined by the student of dreams is one which we all at times tried to solve for ourselves: where does the actual border-line lie? For we never know the moment when we cross over it, or even the moments when we approach it most nearly. In childhood, and long after childhood ended, most of us have tried very hard, but tried in vain, to keep a watch so vigilant, as we approached the border, that we should know the moment of our crossing it.

It is indeed strangely tantalising that this mystery of sleep should happen nightly, without our getting any nearer to a consciousness of its actual oncoming. Every night our normal mind abdicates its power, and the dream mind comes to its own, waking into activity, and taking the reins into its own hands. But the moment of that mysterious transition is always effectively veiled from us. The nearest I have ever been able to get to a realisation of it has been when I have been reading rather late into the night. Sleep is approaching; the dream mind has already started on its activities and has set in motion a train of thought or dream story. The page of the book that I am reading still lies open before my eyes, and though it is becoming rather indistinct, it has not yet wholly gone from my sight; my mind is fast "losing hold," but I am not yet asleep. Suddenly, as though it were in the middle of the printed page, I read a sentence which does not belong there at all, an alien sentence wholly disconnected from the subject or sense of the book. To what does this belong? I am conscious that it has come from elsewhere, that it was part of a definite sequence of ideas or story which was being carried on on another "floor" of my mind, by another part of my brain. This story or thread of ideas was interrupted by the normal mind momentarily resuming its functions and supremacy. The two quite different strains of thought which were being carried on simultaneously have crossed each other, and I am for the moment aware of both. One night when this occurred, the book I was reading lay at a little angle to my eyes and I noticed that, whilst this made the lines of the printed page slope upwards from left to right, the interposed alien sentence seemed to be written at an obtuse angle to these, cutting diagonally across the printed lines. "It is like a weaver's warp and woof," I thought; and this is indeed the truest image that can be made of these interwoven and crossing strands of thought. Instances of such interweaving could be multiplied indefinitely by anyone sufficiently interested to make note of them at once, but the memory of the interposed idea is so evanescent that it fades away with extreme quickness and cannot be recalled. Drifting slowly towards sleep one night I was thinking over some public work that had taken up all the time and energy of the day. Suddenly across these thoughts there "came through" a clear-cut sentence belonging to a wholly different set of ideas, intercepted—as a scrap of a conversation is overheard on the telephone, or a portion of an alien "wireless" message is "tapped" by a Marconi operator. The intercepted fragment ran thus: "Haunted by the pirate ship." For one instant before the memory of it faded out I remembered the context that this belonged to; I remembered a ship with sails. I knew that it was somehow connected with piracy on the high seas, and that the story had to do with ships engaged in the oil-carrying trade, but the memory of it all faded away almost instantaneously, as indeed always happens; only the words of the intruding sentence remaining for a little while printed on my mind.

Another similar note was made at about the same hour of the night. My mind had been dwelling on the anxieties of the war and on certain war work that was occupying me. The words that "came through" were as remote as they well could be from these thoughts; they were—"newly fledged birds on a tree—all grey," and with these words, just for one brief second, the picture they referred to also came back. I remembered a row of very tiny birds perched on a grey bough—"not a tree," I said to myself, "it was a bough only." They were small fluffed-out things, their breasts ruffled by a little gust of wind which disturbed the downy feathers, making little waves like the waves that the wind makes when lightly blowing over grass. "All grey and white," I thought, "and the bough grey too." And then I realised that all this was an intercepted bit, taken out of quite a different train of thought, and that the context to which the words and the grey picture belonged had wholly disappeared.

It is probably true that, not only in the twilight time between sleeping and waking, but also by day, the mind and the subconscious mind are often at work simultaneously on different trains of thought; but if this be the case the normal mind is generally so dominant that no message can penetrate through to interrupt it; and only at times, when a drowsy condition causes it to lose its grip and mastery, can the working of the subconscious mind be perceived. The rare moments when we thus become aware of this duplicate working may have a certain value in the study of dreams, and we have to glean what we can from them, for the difficulty of tracing dream origins is great, and the sources of our knowledge about the dream mind are so limited that we cannot afford to disregard any clue that may give us further insight into them.

There are, for instance, many dreams whose central idea is gathered from a book, generally a book that has lately been read, or that we are reading at the time. The book, like everything else that the dream mind makes use of, will be completely metamorphosed; but some leading idea or some character taken from it will be carried on into the dream. It is sometimes possible to study the actual process by which this is effected in the state where waking and sleeping shade into one another.

I was reading late at night one of Arnold Bennett's chronicles of English midland life, and as I read sleep must have approached. Between sleeping and waking my mind wandered from the book, and a new and different story superimposed itself and ousted the other. The hero of the book remained the principal actor; his name and characteristics were unchanged, but he was placed in an entirely new setting. A wild and unsettled prairie country with steeply undulating outlines now made the background of his adventures. Great caves with ramifying passages sheltered a group of men—pursued or pursuing—against whom he was pitted in a fierce but unequal struggle. I took no part personally in the drama, but was following it step by step, when the thread of it broke suddenly. The light in the room seemed to grow brighter; my eyes still rested on the open page where the hero's name lay before me. For the moment the prairie setting was so much more present to me than the scenery of the "Five Towns" that I could not convince myself quickly that it was not to be found in the book at all and was simply the creation of the dream mind, although sleep had not actually closed my eyes. The intensification of light had acted, as it so often does, as a warning signal just when the moment of true sleep was approaching, and the story that belonged to the borderland of dreams was brought to an abrupt close.

Now, these methods of the dream mind, the qualities of its imagination its habit of seizing upon part of an argument or part of a story to weave into something new and strange, all these are quite unlike the ways of the normal mind that is familiar to me by day. The difference in their methods of working is so sharply defined that I should seldom have to question which was the author of a particular train of thought. They work differently and they arrive at different results; and herein lies undoubtedly a great part of the unexpectedness and charm of the dream mind. We find in it something of the attraction that is to be found in friendship with one whose outlook is not quite like our own and who brings to it qualities of mind that delight us and that are not ours.

CHAPTER XIII

THE ACTORS IN DREAMS
"THE DREAM GUIDE"

And yet, as angels in some brighter dreams
Call to the soul when man doth sleep,
So some strange thoughts transcend our wonted themes
And into glory peep.
—HENRY VAUGHAN, *"They Are All Gone."*

Who is the Guide who comes into so many of my
dreams? Amongst the varied company of people
who take their place in these dreams, this rather
shadowy figure is by far the most persistent.
Some among this company represent the friends of
real life, some are composite portraits, blending the
characteristics of more than one person; whilst others are like the characters of the novelist and seem
to be the inventions of the dreamer's mind. Of all
these figures in my dreams, none takes so constant
a part as the Guide. He seems always to stand close
to me, always a little behind me. I take his presence so entirely for granted, that when he speaks
I do not turn round, or try to see him. I am not
concerned, in my dreams, to question who he is; or
how or why he is possessed of such authority and
knowledge. His wisdom always apparently transcends that possessed by my dream mind; and he

tells me things which in my dreams I do not know. Sometimes he jests, often he laughs; sometimes he laughs at me. Because I have known his judgment to be profounder than my own, he has in certain dreams, calmed my excitement and my fears. In one or two dreams, but not often, I have believed that the Guide's presence was that of a divine messenger; for it has seemed in these dreams that he had a wisdom beyond the wisdom belonging to men. Like all dream students, I have sought to find an answer to the riddle that meets us as soon as we begin to think about dreams— Whence do the actors in our dreams come? If they are the creation of the dream mind alone, how is it that they are able to play all these different parts, and to carry on the dialogue and arguments that they sustain so well?

And, as the Guide enters so constantly into my dream life, these questions have naturally turned upon his personality and origin, and I have asked, Whence does the wisdom of the Guide come? And can he be really the product of my own mind?

Confronted by a similar problem, one writer has advanced the theory that the dramatis personæ in such dreams must come from a source extraneous to the dreamer, since there is no reason why surprise should be experienced if our own mind is the source of the dream content. I should like to believe in this theory, and to feel that the Guide and other dream personalities come from a source external to myself; but I cannot feel any conviction of this; it seems more in harmony with all dream experience to conclude that everything that is contained in dreams —the dream rooms and the dream country in which they take place, as well as the actors in them—are alike the invention of the dreamer's mind.

The wisdom displayed by the Guide, the singular quality of illumination that in dreams he seems to possess, may probably be explained by the heightened powers of the faculty of imagination in the dream and borderland states, to which frequent reference is made in this book. But though this may help to explain the Guide's wisdom, the explanation does not carry us very far. It is still very difficult to conceive the process by which the personages who play their parts on the stage of our dreams are created, and are able to sustain their widely different and consistent rôles.

Certain dream experiences may possibly throw a little light on what is a very difficult problem. There are some dreams in which it seems as though two ''selves,'' or two ''minds'' were at work at the same time, playing different parts, and bringing to their respective parts different mental characteristics. In certain of these dreams we are actually conscious of being present ourselves, in a dual capacity, and of acting in them as D—the dreamer— and as S—myself. (It is thus that I am obliged in making notes of these dreams to distinguish between the two rôles, both of which ''I'' fill.)

The following note gives an example of such a dream, and illustrates the double part which the dreamer fills in them. This particular dream took place near the point of waking, but similar dreams take place at different periods of sleep. In two successive dreams of rather disordered sleep I was preoccupied by the same absurd but nightmareish worry. I thought that certain household possessions, some fine pieces of brocade, and silk curtains, had been left out of doors, and had been found in the rain and melting snow. The care of getting these things dried and restored became an obsession which distracted my dream imagination. In the second part of the dream, when the trouble had become acute, and when I was presumably near to the point of waking, I not only took part as the dreamer, but was present in a double capacity; for "I" interrupted the dream, and argued sternly with the dreamer as to the reality of the trouble that was so oppressive. "I" said, "This is a dream—I am certain of it; you must wake." But the dreamer replied, "It cannot simply be a dream, because it was not only in this dream, but in the dream before this one that I discovered these things in the snow; it must be real, or it would not happen twice, and here are the actual things which you can see and touch for yourself." "I" was very puzzled, and said that "I" could not answer this, or explain it properly; it did indeed seem very real even to me, and very confusing. "I" examined the soiled materials again; they felt very wet and dripping in my hands and seemed to be convincingly "real." "Perhaps," I thought, "some of the seeming facts are really true"—I could not disentangle them from what was

false; only "I" felt sure that a great deal of the
worry was "dream trouble, not day trouble."
"No," the dreamer argued again, "for you can see
and feel the wet things—they are too real to be
'dream things.'" "Well," "I" said at last, "will
you put it to the touch, and test it? Wake," "I"
said, "and see just how much of this is a dream!"
And I woke.

In such a dream as this, we are aware of two
streams of consciousness, both part of ourselves.
It seems as though two factors of a dual consciousness were both actively present, and as though for
the moment we were conscious of two "selves," a
dream "self" and a normal "self," which when we
sleep is subconscious to the dream mind, which seeks
to interfere and to bring in will-power to control,
and reason to guide, the dream imagination.

I suppose that whenever the formula for stopping
or changing a dream is made use of, some such interference with the operation of the dream mind
really takes place, and that this interference is the
secret of dream control.

There are often moments in the transition time
between waking and sleeping when we may become
suddenly aware that both the normal mind and the
dream mind are at work simultaneously.[1] But in
these moments in the borderland state the two operate independently. Two strains of thought cross
each other, we may become aware of both, but they
move on separate lines. When, however, the bor-

[1] Cf. Chapter XII, "Borderland State."

der-line of sleep has been crossed, it is different. When the normal mind, by whatever name we designate this primary self, enters the province that belongs to the dream mind and interferes in it (as it appears at times to do), it seems to act co-operatively, bringing suggestions from without, and importing memories, knowledge of facts, and trains of reasoning, to supplement the imperfect argument and reasoning of the dream. The reasoning thus supplied appears to us in our dreams to come from outside ourselves and to be the more remarkable and convincing. It is only in a few dreams, such as that which has been quoted above, that we are conscious of our dual capacity, and are aware that we are taking the parts both of the "dreamer" and of the other actor; both being, in fact, our very selves. In most dreams I imagine that a similar process is carried out, but without our being aware of it. In the dreams which centre round the Guide, I am never conscious of this division of personality. The Guide does not seem to be myself, but neither do his moral sense and outlook appear to be essentially different from those which are mine by day or those which I aspire to. Although in my dreams I feel him to be possessed of gifts of wisdom belonging to a higher plane than my own, there is fundamental harmony between his ideas and my own waking thoughts. Again, when I analyse the knowledge that he imparts in dreams I see that it comes from sources which are at my command by day, though he often recalls things to my memory which I have totally forgotten. He seems to me always to be more imaginative than myself, and often suggests a train of thought or literary allusion that I have difficulty in tracing.

To give an illustration of the part that the Guide takes in certain dreams I have given here two notes of such dreams. In the first of these the Guide seemed to me in the dream to be a divine messenger. It is one of the few dreams in which I have not taken his presence for granted, and in which I have questioned his origin and the source of his authority. In this dream "I was in a very broad street leading down to the Thames Embankment and was looking out at the river and sky beyond. The Guide was standing just behind me; our hearts were filled with anxiety for the country because of the war, and we were watching there to see what was about to happen. As I watched, I saw on the roadway and tramlines of the Embankment a number of open military wagons coming up filled with men, and gazing at them, I saw to my horror that they were not our own khaki-clad men, but strange soldiers dressed in black with a touch of red on their helmets. 'They are Austrians or Germans,' I exclaimed, and, with the thought that the enemy was here, the bitterness of despair seemed to overwhelm me; all that French women were feeling and suffering would now, I thought, be felt and suffered by ourselves, but the Guide, speaking very low, almost in a whisper, bade me take comfort and look again. 'These are not Germans or Austrians,' he said, 'but soldiers of the

Allies; and see, in the wagons behind them there are English soldiers!'

"The relief was so great that the tears ran down my face, and I stooped down and kissed the English earth. 'But the enemy must be very near,' I thought, 'or all these troops would not be here to defend London,' and for the first time in my life, I, who have always been so glad and thankful for my womanhood, felt that it was hard to have been born a woman—unable to defend my country for which such a passion of love had sprung up in my heart. 'Oh, why was I not made a man, so that I could have been a soldier now!' I cried, and the Guide answered, 'Is that very grateful to Me—you who have borne four sons to serve England—are you not ungrateful?' And I knew that indeed he was right. And then a question about the Guide himself flashed through my mind 'Who are you,' I thought. 'Are you my father that you speak like this—are you God who made me? Are you a Spirit? Who are you?' I thought the Guide laughed very gently, and I turned round quickly, but there was no one there that I could see. 'Oh, where are you?' I cried, for a sort of panic seized me that he had altogether gone, or that he might be hurt in the strife that I thought was surely coming. 'Oh, come!' I called, 'out of this broad street, where there may be fighting soon—it isn't safe here!' and then in a moment it struck me what a comedy it was that I should be so distressed, and in such great fear for the Guide's safety and not for my own, knowing as I did in my heart that he was one whom the enemy had no power to harm at all.

"I stood alone now in the wide empty road, and looked at the tall houses on either side of it. The people living in these houses had clambered out on to the roofs to look at the troops, and to see what would happen. One man seemed to be waving his arms. I thought he might be a spy—or at any rate that he and others ran a great chance of being treated as such—so I called to them as loudly as I could to leave their roofs and go into safety; warning them that if they appeared to be signalling to the enemy, they would be in the gravest danger. I shouted to them, and I persuaded them to go indoors, but I could not help laughing as I watched one stout woman making her way with difficulty back into safety through her attic window. I turned then into a narrow side street, and passed through an archway into one of the houses."

In another dream the Guide had been the witness of the scene he described, and his story was so vivid that I still feel as if I had seen it with my own eyes and had not simply heard it told in a dream.

I had been re-reading Swinburne's "Poems and Ballads," and reading Mr. Gosse's "Life of Swinburne"; and by a natural transition my mind had wandered away at times to Shelley. That night "my dream was of Swinburne's death. The Guide who was with me had himself seen the end; and he told me how the poet had died. Death had come to him, the Guide said, in the midst of war, in a battle-plane high over the fields of France. He felt sure that a bullet had struck the poet; but almost at the same moment the plane had fallen, diving downwards in flames, burning very fiercely. As he described it he made me see vividly the very scene, and the little bright flames against the sky licking up to the burning wings of the plane as it fell. 'And so,' the Guide said—and his words ran in a sort of chant—'Swinburne was happy, as Shelley was happy in his death—Sea and Fire for the one—death above the clouds for the other, a soaring death, and for them both at last Fire.' "

The dream passed on to other scenes of war in France. Waking from it, it was hard to believe that it was not real, that things had not happened so; and hours afterwards, when I copied out the rough shorthand note of the early morning, it seemed easier to believe in the story as it was told to me than to believe in the end that history records—"the motionless existence of the little old genius, and his little old acolyte, in their dull little villa" at Putney.[1]

If it is sometimes hard to believe that the actors who take part in these dreams come, not from without, but from within our own consciousness, the belief is even harder in the case of dreams which seem to give back to us for a little while the presence of those whom we have loved, and who are parted from us. They may come to us in "clear dream and sol-

1 E. Gosse, "Life of Swinburne."

emn vision''—we do not question how they come;
their presence seems for the moment as real as the
comfort that they bring.

> Come to me in my dreams and then
> By day I shall be well again;
> For then the night will more than pay
> The hopeless longing of the day.[1]

There must be many who have sorrowed, who have
found with the wise physician that ''there is a nearer
apprehension of anything that delights us in our
dreams than in our waked senses; without this I
were unhappy; for my awaked judgment discon-
tents me, ever whispering unto me that I am from
my friend; but my friendly dreams in the night re-
quite me, and make me think I am within his
arms.''[2]
The unhappy, the desolate, may still find in
dreams, and only in dreams, the ''certain knot of
peace, the balm of woe'' that Sir Philip Sidney
found in them, when he had fallen on evil days, and
when grief and disappointment had become familiar
to him. In dreams the sorrowful may find the place
that they seek, where pain is stilled, and where for a
little while love may revisit them. And having
found it, they long for a spell which would summon
these ''friendly dreams'' more often. But these are
just the dreams which elude our spells, and over
which the simple rules of dream control that I know

[1] Matthew Arnold.
[2] Sir Thomas Browne.

have no power. Other dreams tend to become more and more obedient to the will, but the power of voluntary dreaming stops short here, and the dreamer has, I believe, little power to call up the dreams that would bring him the greatest comfort. They will come, but not at our bidding; we can only await them, and be grateful for their coming, and for the transient solace that they bring.

But dear and welcome as these dreams are, vivid as they may be, I have never felt about them the conviction that I feel about somewhat similar experiences occurring in the transition time between waking and sleeping and waking—the certainty that they come from "without," not from "within"; the confident sense of the presence of one known to me who, though unseen, is able to communicate clearly and directly with me by channels other than the ordinary channels of sense. Even the most convincing of dreams seem to me to belong to a different plane of experience from this. It is possible that the psychologist may say that he does not recognise such a distinction between mental phenomena on the hither side of sleep and those occurring after its borderland has been crossed. I do not know—the question is full of difficulty—but personally I feel assured that the experiences that I am familiar with in the earlier stage of the borderland state are actually of a very different order from any dreams that I have known. Of the dreams of which I have spoken, I am content to believe that love co-operates with memory, and memory with imagination, in creating them; and, like Sir Thomas Browne, "I do thank God for my happy dreams, as I do for my good rest, for there is a satisfaction in them unto reasonable desires and such as can be content with a fit of happiness." [1]

[1] Sir Thomas Browne, "Religio Medici."

XIV

MORAL SENSE IN DREAMS

Whatsoever things are true, whatsoever things are honest, whatsoever things are just, whatsoever things are pure, whatsoever things are lovely, whatsoever things are of good report; if there be any virtue, and if there be any praise, think on these things.—*Philippians, iv, 8.*

It is an interesting question how far our moral sense in dreams corresponds to the moral sense of our normal life. Our moral sense and moral character have come to us partly by inheritance, and have been modified by training, by the discipline of life, and by the teaching of religion. They have become essential factors of our selves. How far do these moral characteristics survive unchanged in the world of dreams?

There are some great differences in the way in which we regard things in dreams. Most dreamers will agree with me that one of these differences lies in the absence from the dream mind of any deep sense of responsibility. It is to this freedom from the cares of responsibility that a great part of the sense of pleasure in dreams is due; we have the freedom that a child has from the sense of responsibility and duty that rules the activities of our life by day, and this characteristic of the dream state

173

naturally affects to a certain extent the character of our moral sense in it. There are other very marked differences in the moral sense in the two states.

Great stress is laid by the Freudian school on the recognised fact that we may find ourselves confronted in dreams by thoughts and expressions of emotion that we do not choose to admit to our thoughts in our waking life; ideas which are banished more or less instinctively from our minds. The teachers of this school insist that the repression of these conceptions by day drives these undesirable conceptions into the unconscious mind, whence they will find expression in dreams and will operate in them with greatly increased power. No one will deny the fact that natural emotions which are unduly repressed are apt to take their revenge by poisoning the mind. We have only to read of the results of such repression in the case of the hermits and recluses of old to see how bad, both for the normal and the dream life, such unnatural repression of man's ordinary instincts and emotions can be. I feel sure, however, that the amplifications and illustrations of this theory by Freud, and by the psycho-analysts who follow in his steps, are only partially true, and may be very misleading. They proceed on the assumption that the inhibition or repression of thoughts by day gives to such thoughts a greater power over the dream mind, and that, no matter how completely they are controlled by day, they cannot be controlled in our dreams. It would follow from this argument that there is a field of mental experience which is wholly removed from the control of the moral sense.

I believe that the theory and practice of dream control furnish an answer to this argument. All that I would say here is that we need not necessarily give up the direction of our dreams in this way. If dreams visit us that we do not welcome, or that we do not choose should intrude upon us, a simple rule will free us from them, if we are sufficiently determined about the matter. It is after all a matter of will. To forbid, and prevent the recurrence of, an undesired dream is a comparatively easy task, by methods that have been described in Chapter I of this book. In order to give an example of this I have taken from my notes some that relate to "dreams of anger."

A sense of anger, which I have very rarely felt by day, used at times to enter into my dreams as an emotion more violent of its kind than I ever remember having felt in my waking life. The occasion was generally some very trivial one, which excited, however, an unnatural degree of passion in my dream mind. These dreams suggested an experiment in dream control which I carried out. Hereafter, when the sensation of anger came into a dream, it brought automatically with it the associated memory of the formula by which I arrest a dream's course, and control was thus established. In such a dream which I recorded I had become very angry—so angry that I wished to strike the offending person who had aroused my wrath. At this moment the formula interposed itself, and I knew that this was a dream, and realised that it was "dream anger" that I felt. A reflected memory of the description given by Mr. Havelock Ellis of inhibition of the power of movement in dreams flashed at the same time into the dream mind. "If this is only a dream and only dream anger," I said to myself, "you will have no power to strike" The muscular power that I had been conscious of possessing an instant before, and that I had been ready to use, was indeed no longer mine. "Yes," I thought, "then it must be really a dream, and really dream anger"; and I awoke.

When the nature of these dreams had been fully recognised they tended to occur less and less often. I think that the recognition acted as a warning that the impulse of foolish wrath was latent in my mind, and must be watched and controlled by day as well as by night. I am convinced that if we recognise frankly an impulse that our moral sense condemns, such as violent anger, jealousy, or any other passion which belongs to the baser side of our nature, and which offends our moral sense, the control of such impulse by day tends in course of time to eliminate it from our dreams.

There will, however, still be dreams that may trouble us with suggestions of lower emotions and passions, which do not consciously form a part of our normal thought, or which have been eliminated from it—the "repressed thoughts" that the teaching of Freud has explained. Children growing up are often startled by experiencing in dreams emotions, the origin and meaning of which are unknown to them; and, long after childhood and adolescence are passed, dreams of emotions which would not be admitted to normal consciousness may be experienced. It is well to face all the facts about our nature; an ostrich-like attitude towards them will only leave us ignorant and defenceless. Recognition of these facts gives us increased power over our emotions and increased assurance in dealing with their manifestations both in the normal and in the dream life. What our thoughts are by day we can more or less decide; we need never be at the mercy of chance thoughts, unless we have abandoned the steering wheel by which the course of the mind is guided. It is too often assumed that whereas we can thus direct the activity of the normal mind, we are at the mercy of any emotion or passion in our dreams. I am sure that this is not really the case.

Teachers of every age and creed, from St. Paul and St. Augustine to Professor William James, have taught in varying language the same lesson—that the impulses and passions of men may be controlled by their will, that base thoughts may be inhibited, driven out by the substitution of nobler ideas. Such repression of base thoughts and such direction of the mind into other channels tends to give us not only the guidance of our thoughts by day, but helps also to decide the nature of our dreams. And even if from time to time unwelcome thoughts, that belong to a lower side of our nature, should reappear, we need not be too much troubled, nor think that the province of dreams lies wholly beyond our control.

We may, if we will, achieve a substantial harmony between these two mental provinces; between our thoughts and actions by day, and our thoughts and actions in dreams, and in a complete and ordered life the two states would tend to approach each other more nearly. Characteristic differences there will always be between them; but these differences would lie, not in a violent antithesis of moral sense, but in such differences as exist between two persons who, differing from each other in many ways, have nevertheless much in common and who agree in the essentials of outlook and conduct.

It is only when dreams of terror, dreams of grief, and dreams of evil have ceased to have power over us that we are able thoroughly to enjoy our dream life; for it is only then that we are able to embark with entire confidence on the nightly adventure of our dreams, and to explore the unknown and delightful country to which they lend us the key.

PRINTED IN THE UNITED STATES OF AMERICA

Made in the USA
Middletown, DE
08 September 2019